Building Learning Power

helping young people become better learners

Guy Claxton

TLO Limited
Bristol

First published in Great Britain in 2002
by TLO Limited
Henleaze House, Harbury Road, Bristol BS9 4PN.

Reprinted with minor corrections 2005.

ISBN 1 901219 43 7

Introduction

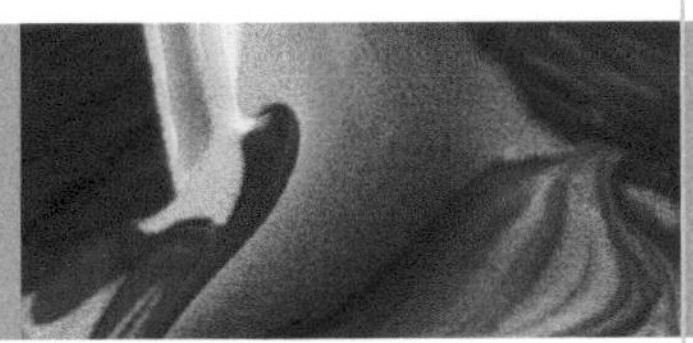

This book is about how teachers can help young people become better learners, both in school and out. It is about creating a climate or a culture in the classroom—and in the school more widely—that systematically cultivates habits and attitudes that enable young people to face difficulty and uncertainty calmly, confidently and creatively. *Building Learning Power* explains what this means and why it is a good idea, and introduces some of the small, do-able things that busy teachers can do to create such a climate.

Students who are more confident of their own learning ability learn faster and learn better. They concentrate more, think harder and find learning more enjoyable. They do better in their tests and external examinations. And they are easier and more satisfying to teach. Even a small investment in building learning power pays handsome dividends for a school. But it also prepares youngsters better for an uncertain future. Today's schools are educating not just for exam results but for lifelong learning. To thrive in the twenty-first century, it is not enough to leave school with a clutch of examination certificates. You have to have learnt how to be tenacious and resourceful, imaginative and logical, self-disciplined and self-aware, collaborative and inquisitive.

So *Building Learning Power* is for anyone who wants to know how to get better results and contribute to the development of real-life, lifelong learners—both at once. In other words, it is for teachers, advisers, teacher trainers, parents and anyone else involved in formal or informal education. It is particularly for people who want more than sound-bites and quick fixes. Some of the early approaches to 'learning to learn' were appealing but unsatisfying. They were built on shaky scientific foundations, and they did not lead to cumulative growth in students' real-life self-confidence or ingenuity. Building learning power—BLP—is firmly grounded in both solid science and practical experience; it takes root and develops over time, and its results are therefore all the more robust.

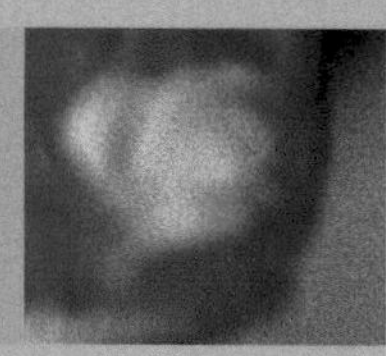

Author's Acknowledgements

There are many people the world over whose pioneering work on learning-to-learn has strongly influenced my own approach. Those abroad include Ian Mitchell and his colleagues at the PEEL project in Victoria, Australia; Elena Kravtsova, grand-daughter of LS Vygotsky, and the staff of the wonderful Golden Key schools in Russia, David Perkins and the late Ann Brown of Harvard, and Carol Dweck of Columbia University, New York. At home, I have to thank all those at Christ Church Primary School in Bradford-on-Avon whose enthusiastic participation in the ECLIPSE project has taught me so much about the practicability of these ideas: headteachers Peter Mountstephen and Beverley Ball, the teachers, especially Carol Craft, Helen Daniels, Kate Drew, Karen Gostick, Sarah Jackson, Liz Ladd and Frances Wills, the parents, especially Chair of the PTA Alison Eveleigh, the governors, and the children, who taught us about learning. From LEAs around the UK I have received particular encouragement and support from Ros Pollard and Hugh Knight in Cardiff, Joan Brown and John Bird in Staffordshire, Gillian Rodd and Graham Cotgreave in Cornwall, and Sharon Cousins, Trevor Coffey and Carmel Gallagher in Northern Ireland. Chris Watkins at the Institute of Education in London has been unfailingly generous with his ideas and materials, as well as his friendship. Bill Lucas stimulated my thinking and kindly invited me to join the Advisory Board for the Campaign for Learning's Learning to Learn project, from which I learnt a good deal, not least about how my ideas differ from some of the other people's that are around. It is a pleasure to record the influence of my colleagues on the ELLI Project at the University of Bristol, Tricia Broadfoot and Ruth Deakin Crick, on the development of my own thinking over the last two years, and to thank the Lifelong Learning Foundation, and especially its Chief Executive Chris Brookes, for both financial and personal support. Finally, I am very grateful to Maryl Chambers, Graham Powell and Gillian Baxter of TLO for coaching my writing style during the production of this book: I am indebted to them for their help, feedback and sound advice.

Publisher's Acknowledgements

ELLI: The Effective Lifelong Learning Inventory

Special mention must be made of the ELLI Project at the University of Bristol. In 2000, the Lifelong Learning Foundation funded Professor Patricia Broadfoot, Professor Guy Claxton and Dr Ruth Deakin Crick to undertake scientific research into the components of learning power and to develop ways of tracking, assessing and nurturing it in schools and colleges. This empirical research project has produced a tried and tested profile of the key dimensions of learning power and a flexible range of assessment tools—the Effective Learning Profile. These assess learners against those key dimensions, enabling teachers and lecturers to see the impact of their teaching on young people's effectiveness as learners: teachers can modify their teaching in response to individual student needs, and so foster the habits of lifelong learning. The research has also identified some of the important ways in which learning power can be nurtured in the classroom. This scientific enquiry into the concept of learning power refines and develops some of the ideas expressed in this book. TLO is looking forward to working with the University of Bristol and the Lifelong Learning Foundation to secure the successful dissemination of this valuable data, and to propagate the fruits of this research in future BLP publications.

And finally:

Our thanks are due to Dean Purnell and Andy Shaw of TLO's publishing studio for their resilience and resourcefulness while working through many drafts of the text; and to Neil Mander of Fruit Design and Marketing Ltd, and once more to Dean and Andy, who together developed the design concept and artwork.

Contents

Section 1a

Powerful learners and their learning minds

Meet Darren and Katie: powerful learners in the making

In this section you will meet Darren, an 11-year-old who already shows many of the habits, traits and attitudes of the effective learner; and Katie, a 17-year-old who is only just discovering how useful they are. We watch Darren as he prepares himself for his first day at his new comprehensive school, and Katie as she discovers and strengthens her ability to think and plan her studies independently. And we look back on their summer holidays, and see how they both tackled various learning challenges. Through these vignettes, you will get a feel for the kinds of things that learning power consists of, and what a difference it makes in real life.

imagining

being absorbed

researching

reflecting

stickability

noticing

questioning

resourcefulness

self knowledge

playfulness

reasoning

collaborating

listening

imitating

Meet Darren and Katie: powerful learners in the making

Darren has gone to bed but he is not asleep. He is imagining what tomorrow will be like—his first day at St Edmund Comprehensive School. It's a big day, and he feels a bit apprehensive. But he has prepared himself as well as he can. He has done lots of research on what St Edmund's is going to be like. Leon's sister Tania is in Year 9 and had Mr Andrews as her tutor too, and when Darren was round at Leon's he had pestered Tania with questions about what the school was like. 'What do you wish you had been told when you first arrived?' he had asked, and Tania told him and Leon all kind of useful things, from the best place to eat your lunch when it's wet, to which of the Year 11s to avoid, and who was the most entertaining maths teacher. He had badgered her to fish out for him some of her Year 7 workbooks, so he could see what kind of work to expect. He was surprised to see that some of it looked just like work that he had done with Mrs Rowe in Year 5. He felt both relieved, and disappointed.

Darren thinks back to his first day at Beckley Road Primary, and how he had felt then—pretty scared to begin with, but by the time he had been there a fortnight, he felt so at home that he wondered what all the fuss had been about. St Edmund's was definitely going to be a bigger challenge—but he knows that he is a much better learner now than when he was five. At Beckley Road all the teachers had talked a lot about learning, and how to become a better learner. They had had lots of discussions about what Mrs Rowe called 'knowing what to do when you don't know what to do', and they had had fun, as a class, making posters for the walls full of suggestions about what to do when you couldn't read a word, or figure out where you had gone wrong in a sum, or had fallen out with someone and wanted to be friends again.

Every Friday afternoon they had had time to write in their 'learning diary'—what Ms Salbiah in Year 6 had called 'My Journey Into The Unknown'—about how their learning had gone during the week, what they had found hard, and what new learning methods they had discovered. Ms Salbiah had written all kinds of thoughtful comments and questions, and as he's thinking about the challenge of the new school, he can hear Ms Salbiah's voice in his head, suggesting that he write down a list of his 'hopes, fears and expectations' so he can compare these with what he actually found. He is so used to doing 'Predict—Observe—Explain' that he hardly needs the voice to remind him now. Darren switches the light back on, picks up the journal that he keeps by the bed, and writes for a few minutes. Having prepared himself as much as he can, he closes the book, turns out the light, and quickly falls asleep.

Katie is downstairs cleaning her kit and thinking about stress. Darren's big half-sister is seventeen, a fitness freak, and studying leisure management at the local college. She has an essay to write over the summer on stress and exercise for her Human Biology module, and she is feeling stressed all right: it has to be in by the end of the week and she's hardly started. She wishes she had paid more attention at school to the stuff on 'independent learning'. She could do with it now, but at the time thought it was a load of rubbish. Seeing how Darren has changed, she's not so sure. He seems so curious and confident these days—not like the

Meet Darren and Katie . . .

wobbly character that she had been at his age, skilfully hiding behind a veneer of 'cool'. If she had felt better equipped to learn, she wouldn't have had to put so much energy into pretending she didn't care. Oh well. It's never to late to learn to learn, Darren had said. Hope he's right.

Actually, Katie has already started to develop her 'learning muscles' (being a fitness fanatic, she likes the metaphor). She realises that 'No pain, no gain' applies just as much to learning as it does to running on the treadmill—so a bit of 'brain-stretching' doesn't mean she's thick, it just means she's learning. Even this realisation has enabled her to stick at things better. As she reminds herself of this, her panic about the essay begins to subside, and she starts thinking about it again. Of course she's supposed to write about the biological view of stress—it's what happens when you push a system to its limits—and about how exercise makes your system more 'elastic' so it can cope with more demands. But maybe if some people think that getting hot and sweaty means they're weaklings (just like she thought 'trying' meant she was stupid), that makes exercise itself stressful. Ha! she thinks, that's an angle that Rob George, her tutor, won't have thought of. And leaving her stuff to soak in the sink, she sits down to write a plan of what she might look up in the library tomorrow to develop her idea.

Over the summer the whole family—Katie and Darren, as well as Darren's dad Charlie, Katie's mum Miriam and their new baby brother Franklin—had been on holiday to one of the Greek islands. Darren had been into everything, and had had the time of his life. Charlie had remarked to Miriam that Darren was indeed a different child from the five-year-old who wouldn't let go of his hand on his first day at Beckley Road. For a year or two after he and Darren's mum had separated, he had been very timid and withdrawn, but to see him snorkelling out of his depth, and chattering away with the two German girls in some strange hybrid language that the kids seemed to have invented, you would never have known it.

If Darren wanted to master something, there was no stopping him now. He had even joined in with the Greek dancing classes in the evening, quite unafraid of making a fool of himself, and dancing with strangers in the group apparently without a care in the world. Charlie had been particularly impressed by the quiet way he had stood and just watched people doing what he wanted to do for a while before trying it out. It was as if he drank their skill in through his eyes, and his brain had already half-learned it before he set foot on the dance floor himself. It was almost, thought Charlie, as if Darren had somehow recovered the natural learning flair that he—and, he supposed, nearly all children—had had as a toddler.

It was infectious too: even Katie had let go a bit. She had done her usual sulk all the way to the airport ('I don't know why I let you talk me into this stupid holiday. I'm an adult. I don't do holidays with parents!') But then there she was, practising her rather ungainly diving off the side of the boat, surrounded by a gaggle of boys half her age, with a most uncharacteristic mixture of enthusiasm, persistence and unselfconsciousness.

Not to mention daring to practise her rudimentary Greek in the taverna in the evenings.

Yes, Charlie was a little envious of their—what did Darren call it?—'learning power'. He even admitted ruefully to himself that he often played the fool and made cynical comments on training days, rather than risk making a mistake or asking a question that might seem silly. He would rather sneak off and read the manual in his hotel room overnight than join in with the group tasks they were set. (He remembered sheepishly having done the same thing with the Rubik cube that Darren had brought home, secretly studying the instructions rather than just messing about with it, as Darren had done.) Yet at work his life seemed more and more to involve project work, learning, and problem-solving together in teams of very disparate people. He admired both Katie and Darren's ability to create and develop playful projects with the other youngsters at the hotel, even when they did not speak each other's languages.

Of course even Darren still had his down times and disappointments. Learning for him wasn't all sweetness and light. He got frustrated and dispirited, confused and apprehensive, sometimes. But Charlie was amazed at how quickly he bounced back. Darren's old headteacher at Beckley Road had explained, one parents' evening, that they deliberately aimed to teach students how to deal with the emotional side of difficulties and upsets, so that they could be in charge of their own recovery. Charlie had thought at the time that it sounded rather touchy-feely, but he had to admit that it worked for Darren.

And now it's a bright September morning. Darren in his new school uniform and Katie in her designer sweat-suit are grabbing a bowl of cereal and getting their things together. Katie is off to the library to see what she can find on the relationship between self-esteem, body-image and attitudes to exercise—bit of a mouthful, but she's quite gripped by the idea. And Darren has to hurry to meet Leon for their walk to St Edmund's. 'OK, mate?' says Charlie to Darren as he flies out of the door. 'Bit wobbly, Dad' he calls back, 'but I'll be fine.' And Charlie thinks to himself 'Yes, you will.'

Section 1b

Powerful learners and their learning minds

Developing the mind to learn

This section explains how building learning power (BLP) differs from, and goes beyond, other 'learning to learn' approaches. It gives a systematic introduction to the mind of the effective learner, in terms of the four Rs of resilience, resourcefulness, reflectiveness and reciprocity. By the end of the section, you will have a clear all-round picture of the habits of mind that BLP aims to cultivate.

Key points

- Know what's worth learning
- Know what you're good at learning
- Know who can help
- Know how to face confusion
- Know the best learning tool for the job

Getting learning fit

Imagine a tennis player getting ready for a match. She practises specific shots and abilities—but she also works on her general stamina, strength and coordination, and she tries to develop her self-awareness and her ability to be strategic. She makes sure that her body and mind are as fit and sharp as can be. BLP is about helping young people develop this kind of general, all-round, learning fitness and readiness. It's not just about teaching them a narrow set of learning techniques.

To work on fitness, you don't spend all your time in the gym on one exercise or one piece of equipment. You follow a balanced, varied work-out regime that relies on proven knowledge about muscle groups and the cardiovascular system. Likewise, BLP uses our knowledge of learning and the mind to create a coherent picture of the kinds of mental agility and emotional stamina the good learner has, and to make sure that schools give all these aspects the work-outs they need in order to develop.

RESEARCH TELLS US . . .

High achievers are not necessarily good real-life learners

Resilience in the face of difficulty is one of the most basic ingredients of learning power. Yet apparently you can be successful in school without it. Carol Dweck of Columbia University gave a maths test to a mixed-ability group of 14-year-old girls. In the middle of the test booklet, for some of the girls, had been stapled, as if by accident, a page of problems that none of them knew how to do. On the (perfectly do-able) problems after the impossible ones, many of the high-achieving girls did very poorly. As a result of being temporarily flummoxed, they had gone to pieces. These successful students were woefully lacking in resilience, and so could not really be classed as good overall learners.

Developing the mind to learn

Darren and Katie are, of course, fictitious, and Darren in particular is something of an ideal. Nobody can be an exemplary learner all of the time. But everyone can learn to be a better learner, more of the time—not just in school but in the whole of life. Darren has learned to become a stronger, more confident and more competent learner, and Katie is on the way. We now know that 'learning to learn' is a real possibility. How well you learn is not a matter of how bright you are. It is a matter of experience, and good coaching. There is a lot of talk about learning at the moment, and the goal of enhancing students' learning is widely espoused. In practice, though, this can mean one of three rather different things. First, it can mean helping students to *learn more*, and thus raise their achievement. To do this, you might offer incentives, or cut the syllabus into small, bite-sized pieces that make it easier to ingest. Secondly, you can help students to *learn better*. That might mean helping them find out what is their preferred learning style, and taking that into account as you teach; or making sure that students are well fed and watered before lessons. Thirdly, you can try to help students to become *better learners*—not just in school but in real life as well. That might mean trying to help them develop the skills and attitudes to learn well whatever the conditions.

These three goals are not the same, and methods that work for one don't always suit the others. Spoon-feeding may improve results, but it doesn't develop chewing muscles. It is quite possible to help students learn more without helping them become better at learning. Indeed, some ways of raising achievement actually damage or undermine students' learning ability. And helping people learn better is also not the same thing as helping them become better learners.

You can help them learn better by providing lots of support and guidance—but when you take that guidance and support away, have they become more independent, or less?

There is a great deal of information and advice around about how to help students learn more or learn better. This book is different. It is about how to develop students as learners—how to increase their portable learning power—and to raise standards by doing so. We call this *building learning power*, BLP. The evidence is: helping students learn more or better does not necessarily help them become better learners. But if you help students become better learners their achievement rises. And they will take away from school not just a few certificates, but greater confidence, competence and curiosity to face the uncertainties that life will surely throw at them. Give your car a good service and it will naturally go further and faster. Aim at levering up standards, and you may get better results, but at the cost of turning out young people who do not know how to think for themselves.

It is obvious from the vignettes that being a good learner is not just a matter of learning a few techniques like mind mapping or brain gym. It is about the whole person: their attitudes, values, self-image and relationships, as well as their skills and strategies. Being a good real-life learner means knowing what is worth learning; what you are good (and not so good) at learning; who can help; how to face confusion without getting upset; and what the best learning tool is for the job at hand. Just as being a reader involves much more than simply being able to read, so 'being a learner' means enjoying learning, and seeing yourself as a learner, seeking out learning as well as knowing how to go about it.

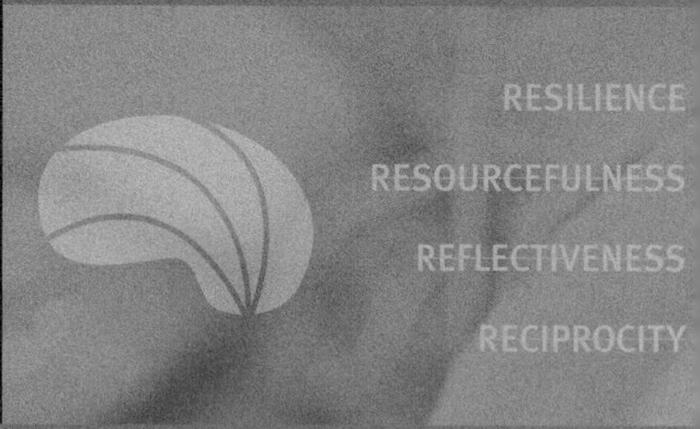

The learning-power mind

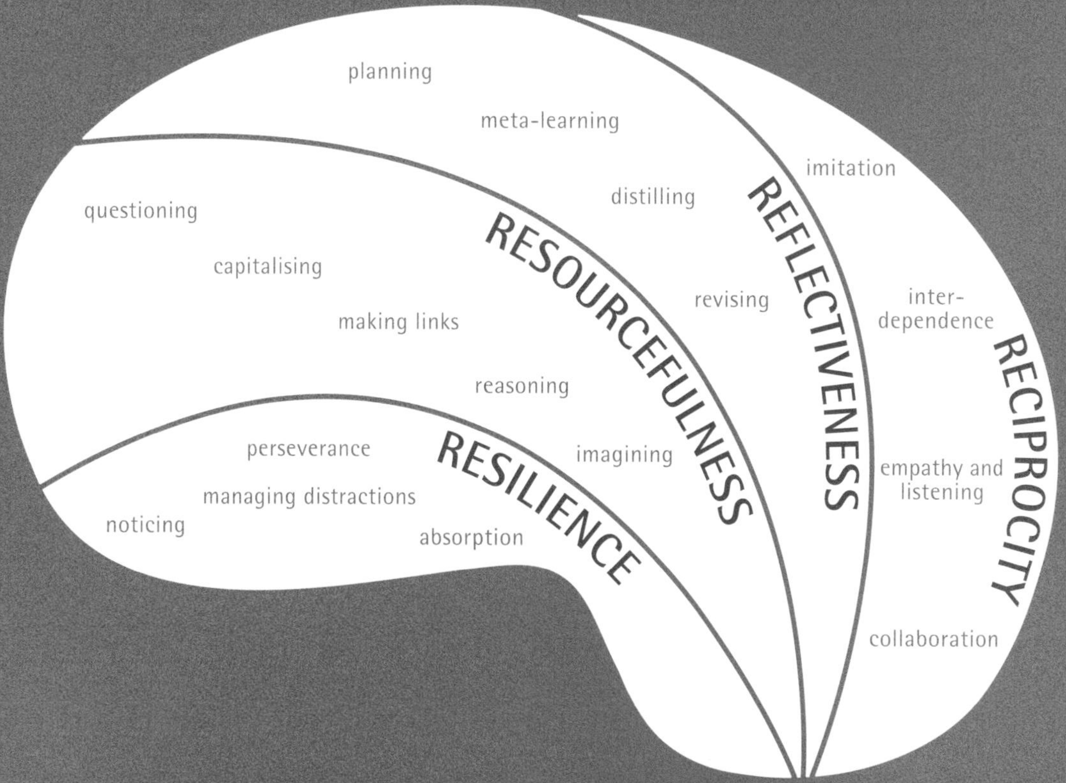

RESILIENCE
perseverance
managing distractions
noticing
absorption

RESOURCEFULNESS
questioning
capitalising
making links
reasoning
imagining

REFLECTIVENESS
planning
meta-learning
distilling
revising

RECIPROCITY
imitation
inter-dependence
empathy and listening
collaboration

Developing the mind to learn . . .

Developing learning power means working on four aspects of students' learning. The first task is to help them become more **resilient**: able to lock on to learning and to resist distractions either from outside or within. The second is helping them become more **resourceful**: able to draw on a wide range of learning methods and strategies as appropriate. The third is building the ability to be **reflective**: to think profitably about learning and themselves as learners. And the fourth task is to make them capable of being **reciprocal**: making use of relationships in the most productive, enjoyable and responsible way.

THE FOUR Rs of LEARNING POWER

Resilience	–	**being ready, willing and able to lock on to learning**
Absorption	–	flow; the pleasure of being rapt in learning
Managing distractions	–	recognising and reducing interruptions
Noticing	–	really sensing what's out there
Perseverance	–	stickability; tolerating the feelings of learning
Resourcefulness	–	**being ready, willing and able to learn in different ways**
Questioning	–	getting below the surface; playing with situations
Making links	–	seeking coherence, relevance and meaning
Imagining	–	using the mind's eye as a learning theatre
Reasoning	–	thinking rigorously and methodically
Capitalising	–	making good use of resources
Reflectiveness	–	**being ready, willing and able to become more strategic about learning**
Planning	–	working learning out in advance
Revising	–	monitoring and adapting along the way
Distilling	–	drawing out the lessons from experience
Meta-learning	–	understanding learning, and yourself as a learner
Reciprocity	–	**being ready, willing and able to learn alone and with others**
Interdependence	–	balancing self-reliance and sociability
Collaboration	–	the skills of learning with others
Empathy and listening	–	getting inside others' minds
Imitation	–	picking up others' habits and values

Key points

Good learners –

- like a challenge
- know that learning is sometimes hard
- are not afraid of making mistakes
- like the feel of learning

The learning-power mind

Resilience

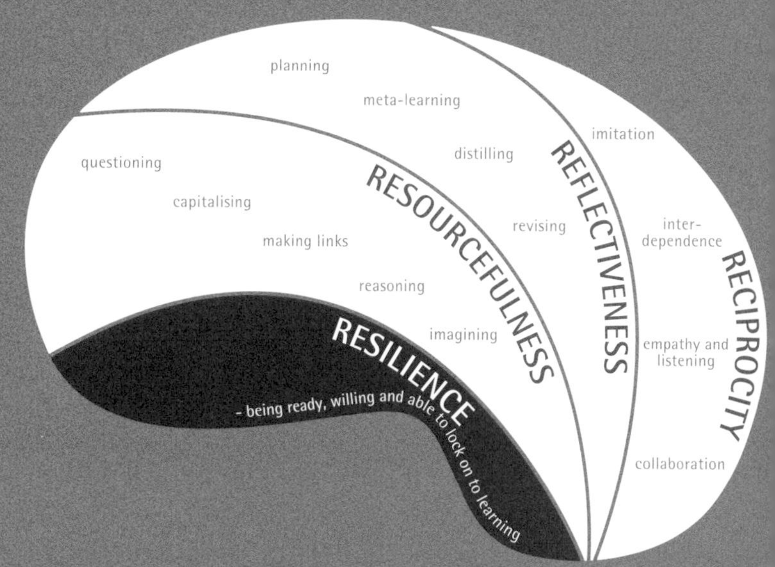

absorption	flow, the pleasure of being rapt in learning
managing distractions	recognising and reducing interruptions
noticing	really sensing what's out there
perseverance	stickability, tolerating the feelings of learning

Resilient: ready, willing and able to lock onto learning

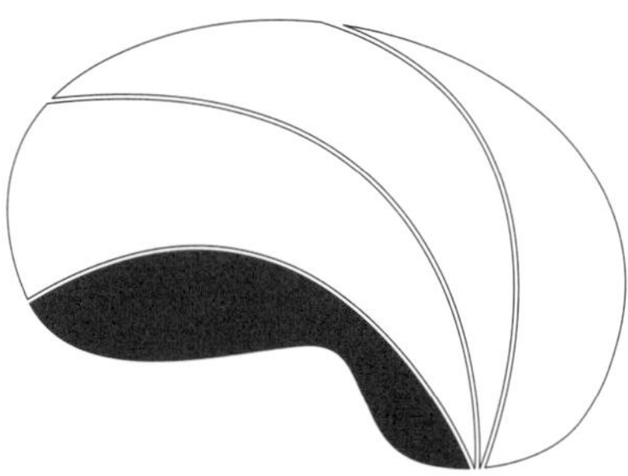

The first aspect of a supple learning-powered mind is the most basic. Resilience is about locking on to learning: being able to get absorbed, and to stay engaged despite external distractions (unless they are genuinely important, of course!); and despite the ebb and flow of the different feelings of learning, such as excitement, frustration or confusion. If good learners do get upset and break off, they are quicker to come back and try again. They are drawn to learning and they like a challenge. They are more likely to 'give it a go' even though the method and the outcome may be uncertain. They know that learning is sometimes hard—for everyone, no matter how 'bright'—and are not generally frightened of finding things difficult or making mistakes. They like the *feel* of learning, as well as the satisfaction of mastering a skill or solving a problem.

There are four aspects to resilience: **absorption**—being rapt in the flow of learning; **managing distractions**—recognising and reducing interruptions; **noticing**—seeing and sensing what's out there; **perseverance**—stickability, tolerating the feelings of learning.

Absorption

For learning to occur, the learner has first to be engaged with the object of learning. They have to be paying attention. But we can pay attention in different ways. Sometimes attention is very focused, deliberate and conscious. Sometimes it is more a kind of background awareness that may not be very conscious at all. This latter kind of attention is not to be underestimated. A lot of learning happens incidentally, out of the corner of your eye, as it were, while you are trying to get something else done. So paying attention does not necessarily mean effortful concentration. The best kind of attention depends on what kind of learning you are up to. But without engagement of some kind, no learning can happen.

If we were merely concerned with raising achievement, we would look for ways to induce the kinds of attention we want—by making lessons more entertaining, maybe, or by chiding students who aren't concentrating. But BLP asks:

How can we systematically help students to develop the habits and dispositions of 'good attending' for themselves, so that over time they become second nature?

Developing learning power means strengthening the ability to pay attention to what is going on, and to maintain attention despite a variety of competing attractions. There are three important things to remember about attention. First, you can't make yourself attend. It's not a matter of talking to yourself, or fixing your eyes earnestly on the page, or furrowing your brow. We attend to what our brains find novel, interesting,

Key points

Concentration –

- can't be forced
- isn't always useful
- develops with age
- is rewarding

Teaching resilience

'It doesn't help a child to tackle a difficult task if they succeed consistently on an easy one. It doesn't teach them to persist in the face of obstacles if obstacles are always eliminated . . . What children learn best from are slightly difficult tasks which they have to struggle through. Knowing they can cope with difficulties is what makes children seek challenges and overcome further problems.'

Professor Carol Dweck, Columbia University, New York

RESEARCH TELLS US . . .

Flow and learning

Students' success in school depends on how rapt they are while they are studying. Jeanne Nakamura gave a group of high school students a small beeper that went off at random times during the day, and when it did, they had to write down what they were doing, and how absorbed or 'in flow' they were feeling. When they were studying, high achieving students reported they were in flow 40% of the time, while low achievers only reported flow 16% of the time. More often, the low achievers were bored or anxious. Comments Daniel Goleman: 'Sadly, the low achievers, by failing to hone the skills that would get them in flow, both forfeit the enjoyment of study, and run the risk of limiting the level of intellectual tasks that will be enjoyable to them in the future.'

Resilient . . .

important, enjoyable, perplexing, disturbing or threatening. To get someone to lock on to learning, the object or activity has somehow to matter to them.

Secondly, distractibility is useful. Being totally immersed in something, however valuable, may mean that you miss whatever else is going on, whether it be a new opportunity or a looming threat. Our ancestors would have been vulnerable if they had not been continually checking for danger, and so, to some extent, are we. Children who have grown up in insecure or chaotic contexts are evolutionarily quite right to be hyper-alert to what is going on around them (constantly on the look-out for potential sources of reassurance, recognition, or further harm). Some students may be preoccupied with much more urgent calls on their attention than the classroom topic of the day.

Thirdly, the ability to maintain concentration on long-term goals, in the face of more immediate attractions, is not finally developed until adolescence. This kind of commitment to our deeper goals and values depends on the frontal lobes of the brain, and we know that these are the last areas of the brain to come fully on line.

For all these reasons we should have realistic expectations of younger or more anxious children. They can't be cajoled or bullied into locking on to learning.

However, having said that,

the ability to get lost in learning is vital, and one we should cultivate. That state of being absorbed, 'rapt', is inherently gratifying and rewarding.

Psychologist Mihaly Csikszentmihalyi says we are programmed to be learning animals partly because the feeling of being stretched by the 'risky edge' of our experience is so exhilarating. Some people get it from skiing or playing an instrument. Some people only get it from such intensely stimulating situations as clubbing or fighting. Others get it from a good book, a crossword puzzle, making models, or a really fast witty conversation (what the Irish call 'the craic'). Good learners like that feeling of absorption, when they're writing an essay just as much as when they're dancing. Teachers can encourage students to recognise and seek that pleasure in all kinds of learning.

Managing distractions

There are things, as we have said, that threaten to disrupt absorption, both from inside and out. If you are hungry, tired or anxious it is hard to concentrate. And so it is if there is too much going on around you, or if you are uncomfortable.

Good learners are aware of possible sources of distraction, and do what they can to diminish them.

Diminishing distractions is an individual matter: what works for one person may not work for another. Some people like to work with background music or sitting on a chair that is not too soft. Others like to lie in bed in the quiet. Good learners find out what their ideal conditions are. Of course, as we saw earlier, not all distractions can be managed so easily. But some can.

Key points

- Learn without thinking
- Contemplate
- Value 'stilling'
- Stick at learning
- Reject undermining false beliefs

The making of a poet

My mother, the scientist, taught me to see. She taught me attention to the complexities of surface detail and also attention to what lies beneath those surfaces . . . In doing so, she made me a poet. My mother, the researcher . . . sat patiently at the microscope on the kitchen table, observing, noticing, discovering patterns, making sense. In that kitchen, I learned the patience of research. My mother made order of the raggedness of the living world, and I was paying attention. I didn't know at the time I was . . . Yet . . . on some level, in some hidden and inarticulate way, I must have been attending and recording extremely well . . .

When I taught high school English and creative writing, I was always searching for ways to bring students into attention, the sort of deep attention that would elicit the capacity for poetry . . . In a homework assignment, I would ask them to 'find a place where there's nothing going on. Sit there for ten minutes and record everything that happens.'

Anne McCrary Sullivan, American poet

RESEARCH TELLS US . . .

Resilience and relationships

How resilient children become depends a lot on their relationships with parents and teachers. For example, children learn not only what is interesting, but how to be interested, and for how long, from the habits of the adults around them. Persistence rubs off from one generation to the next. And the reverse is also true. Doreen Arcus has found that timid and unadventurous children tend to have parents and teachers who are anxious on their behalf, and rescue them prematurely from difficulty. However she also found that the caretakers of timid children did not set them clear limits, so they were often unsure whether it was safe to be adventurous or not. Being gently overseen by a benign but firm supervisor enables youngsters to be less cautious or fearful on their own account, because they have faith that, within the limits, they will come to no great harm.

Resilient . . .

Noticing

Learning often relies on being able to pay attention to what you are interested in: not necessarily thinking about it, just really noticing how it looks, what it is made of, or how it behaves. Many professionals, from poets to scientists to business managers, rely on this quality of attentive noticing: being able to identify the significant detail, or to let an underlying pattern of connections emerge into their minds. Sometimes you have to be patient before the detail or the pattern will reveal itself to you, like looking for sea creatures in a rock pool. And this is a skill that can be strengthened with practice. We often pick up this skill from people around us. Babies very soon learn to work out what their mother is focusing on, and to 'share joint attention' with her. It helps to be around people who are demonstrating this ability to watch carefully and turn their observations into accurate descriptions. Getting a really clear sense of *what*, before starting to think about *how* or *why*, is very useful.

Perseverance

Attention can be broken when learning gets blocked, but good learners have learnt the knack of maintaining or quickly re-establishing their concentration when they get stuck or frustrated. The quality of stickability or perseverance is essential if you are going to get to the bottom of something that doesn't turn out as quickly or easily as you had thought, or hoped.

If you get upset and start to think there is something wrong with you as soon as you get stuck, you are not going to be able to maintain engagement.

Instead all your energy will go into trying to avoid the uncomfortable feeling, and this may mean drifting off into a daydream, creating a distraction, or blaming somebody else.
A great deal of classroom misbehaviour starts this way. If students were better equipped to cope emotionally with the inevitable difficulty of learning, they would mess about less. There is a range of things that teachers can do to strengthen students' stickability.

Perseverance is often undermined by two common and erroneous beliefs. The first is that learning ought to be easy. If learners think that they will either understand something straight away, or not at all, then there is simply no point in persisting and struggling. The second is that bright people pick things up easily, so if you have to try it means you're not very bright. Clearly the idea that effort must be symptomatic of a lack of ability makes persevering an unpleasant experience. Good learners develop perseverance when their parents and teachers avoid conveying these messages, even unwittingly.

Key points

- Be curious and inquisitive
- Be adventurous within clear boundaries
- Don't be afraid of 'don't know' state of mind
- Play with materials and ideas

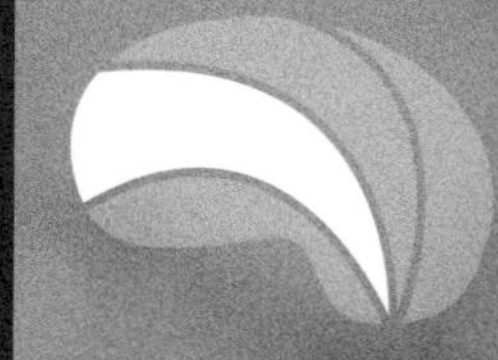

RESILIENCE
RESOURCEFULNESS
REFLECTIVENESS
RECIPROCITY

The learning-power mind

Resourcefulness

questioning	getting below the surface, playing with situations
making links	seeking coherence, relevance and meaning
imagining	using the mind's eye as a learning theatre
reasoning	thinking rigorously and methodically
capitalising	making good use of resources

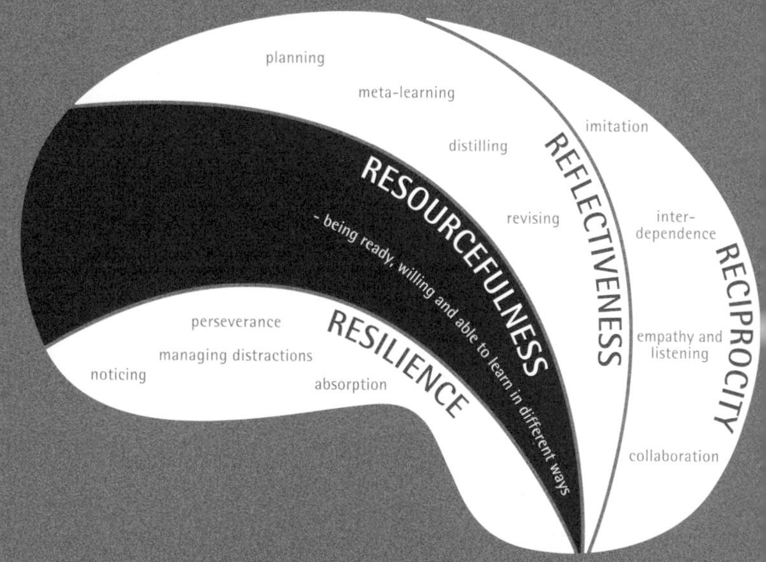

Resourceful: ready, willing and able to learn in different ways

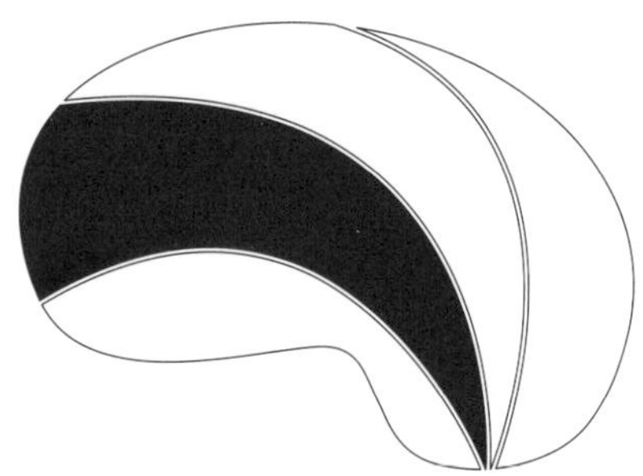

The second aspect of a learning-powered mind is resourcefulness. The great Swiss psychologist Jean Piaget once defined intelligence as 'knowing what to do when you don't know what to do'. Being resourceful means having a good repertoire of attitudes and strategies for confronting the world when it becomes strange or out of control. Good learning involves engaging with uncertainty in effective ways: ways that are most likely to deliver an expanded sense of mastery and comprehension. If resilience is to do with *getting and staying engaged*—with attention and emotion—then being resourceful means being skilful at learning, and having the right frame of mind to want to get to the bottom of things.

Some children's early experience has taught them that the world is not a very comprehensible place, and they may have already developed what psychologists call 'learned helplessness'. They don't bother to look for order or meaning because they have learned that order and meaning are not to be found. Conversely, children become bolder and more curious when their world is full of structure and rhythm which they can easily discover. Success at finding or creating order and meaning encourages them to go on and look for more. The old wisdom about 'freedom within clear boundaries' really does produce more adventurous spirits.

There are five ingredients of resourcefulness: **questioning, making links, imagining, reasoning** and **capitalising.**

Questioning

Questioning means both the ability to ask good questions and the disposition to do so (which is sometimes called curiosity). Good learners like questions, and are not afraid of the 'don't know' state of mind out of which questions emerge.

Good learners like to wonder about things. For them, it often really is a wonder-ful world. The phrases 'How come?' and 'What if?' are never far from their lips.

They value getting below the surface of things, and are less likely to accept uncritically what they are told. They like to come to their own conclusions. They are more willing to reveal their questions and uncertainties if they think it will help them learn.

Questioning can be as much non-verbal as it is verbal. Playing around with materials or ideas just to see what happens is a powerful way of asking questions. It is what artists and inventors spend a lot of their time doing. The inclination to ask questions flourishes when you are around people who are also asking questions, and who encourage and appreciate your questions too.

Key points

- Look for patterns and relationships
- Connect new learning with your opinions and beliefs
- Use 'active' and 'receptive' imagination
- Play with ideas and possibilities

'Students' revision becomes more effective, and their exam results improve, if they spend a little time mentally rehearsing the process of revision before they embark upon it.'

Professor Shelley Taylor, University of California

'He who is afraid of asking is afraid of learning.'

Danish proverb

RESEARCH TELLS US . . .

The power of mental rehearsal

Shelley Taylor at the University of California has shown that imagining yourself revising actually improves examination performance. Shortly before an exam, she asked one group of students to spend five minutes a day imagining themselves revising in a way that would give them a good mark. A second group imagined themselves having done well. And a control group just revised in the normal way. The second group actually studied less than the controls and did worse in the exam, while the first group studied more and improved their marks by an average of eight percentage points.

RESEARCH TELLS US . . .

'Could be' language

Ellen Langer at Harvard University has shown that the teacher's choice of language can make a great difference to students' creativity. She taught two groups the same idea about how cities grow, except for one group she said 'This is how it happens', while the other group she told 'This could be how it happens.' The groups learnt the information equally fast, but when they were asked to use the information in a new way, the 'could be' group easily outperformed the 'is' group. Langer explains that 'could be' language invites students to think how else things might be. 'Is' language simply has to be grasped. If something is the absolute truth, all you can do is try your best to understand and remember it.

Resourceful . . .

There are classrooms that have a 'Wonder Wall' where both students and teachers store up all their questions. There are classrooms where marks are awarded for good questions as well as good answers.

Making Links

The second aspect of resourcefulness is integrating or making links between different things. Again, it comprises not only the ability to see or make relationships but also the inclination to look for them.

Trying to hook up new experiences with what you already know is what some people call 'making meaning'.

New ideas become meaningful to the extent that we can incorporate them within our own mental webs of associations and significances. When the patterns of relationship to be discovered are rather complex or subtle, business guru Peter Senge calls it 'systems thinking'. Good learners get pleasure from seeing how things fit together. They are interested in the big picture, and how new learning expands it.

Good learners can make all kinds of different links. They can link together this lesson's physics topic with what they were doing in maths last week. They can look for links to their own goals and interests, to discover the relevance of the new learning to their own lives. They find links to their own real-life experience—using new ideas or theories to make sense of past impressions. They weave new events into their developing autobiographical story relating them to their sense of self. They can connect new learning with their own opinions and beliefs, so that they come out not just knowing something new, but looking at the world in a different way. And—very importantly for creativity—they may look for analogies in their own memory that give them a handle on a complicated new domain. 'What's it like?' they ask themselves.

Imagining

That brings us on to the third ingredient of resourcefulness: imagining. Imagination is not just a cute faculty that children use to weave fantasies: it is one of the most effective tools in the learner's toolbox. Scientists, designers and executives need a powerful imagination just as much as painters and novelists, and it can either be developed, through appropriate experience and encouragement, or left to shrivel up. Good learners are ready and able to look at things in different ways. They like playing with ideas and possibilities, and adopting different perspectives (even though they may not have a clear idea of where their imagination is leading them). They use pictures and diagrams to help them think and learn.

There are two kinds of imagination: active and receptive. In active imagination, you deliberately create a scenario to run in your mind's eye (just as Darren did when he was trying to anticipate what his first day at his new school would be like). Sports people use this kind of mental rehearsal, and experiments have shown it to be very effective at improving their level of skill.

Key points

- Slip problems to the back of your mind
- Use analytical, disciplined thinking
- Use thinking tools for real-life concerns
- Draw on materials to help learning

More than hard thinking

Learning is not the same thing as thinking. Being a good learner involves more than being a logical, systematic thinker. Most kinds of educational exams test mainly the ability to think explicitly and systematically, though it is only recently that schools have started to try to teach students how to do it well directly. But remembering, explaining and deducing are only three learning skills out of a great many. There is plenty of evidence that good explainers are not necessarily good discoverers, and vice versa. Being able to move flexibly between different modes of thinking: that is what BLP aims to develop.

RESEARCH TELLS US . . .

Education doesn't help you think

It is an uncomfortable fact that much of what is learned in school doesn't transfer to real-life situations. David Perkins of Harvard asked several thousand people to make notes for a discussion on general topics such as the impact of TV violence, and then scored the notes in terms of the number and quality of the arguments considered. High-school drop outs performed as well as high-school graduates; first-year undergraduates performed as well as fourth-year; and beginning graduate students were no different from those completing their PhDs. Perkins concludes: 'Broadly speaking, most educational practice does little to prepare students for reasoning about open-ended issues.'

'Teaching thinking . . . is not an alternative to the standards agenda but a way of taking it forward.'

Professor Michael Barber

Resourceful . . .

The second kind of imagination is more receptive, like daydreaming: letting a problem slip to the back of your mind, and then just sliding into a kind of semi-awake reverie, where the mind plays with ideas and images without much control on your part. Successful learners and inventors know how to make good use of this kind of creative intuition. They are interested in inklings and ideas that just bubble up into their minds.

Reasoning

The next element of resourcefulness is reasoning—the kind of logical, analytical, explicit disciplined thinking that schools often focus on (sometimes to the exclusion of some of the other elements). There is a lot of interest at the moment in ways of teaching thinking, and there are many materials for teaching thinking on the market. In BLP, such 'Show your working' kinds of thinking are a very important part of the good learner's toolkit, but they are not the be-all and end-all of learning. In fact, research suggests that secondary schools have not been very successful at developing students' ability to think logically in real life.

It turns out to be quite difficult to free any kind of thinking or learning skill from its ties to the particular setting and subject matter in which it was originally practised.

Nevertheless, being able to construct logical arguments or make practical use of Venn diagrams, for example, is very useful, and good learners need practice at using such tools in the context of their real-life concerns.

Capitalising

The final aspect of resourcefulness is a little different. It is called capitalising, and it means being on the lookout for materials, resources and forms of support in the environment that can help you in your current learning or problem-solving. Traditional schooling assumes that intelligence is all in the head. But recent studies show that it is much fairer and more accurate to see good learners as people who are ready and able to make intelligent use of all kinds of things around them—floor space, filing cabinets, dictionaries, notebooks, personal organisers, telephones, libraries, e-mail; and, of course, other people (who will feature much more in our fourth aspect). Everyone needs to be good at capitalising on the resources available in the world, so it is obviously a good idea to start developing this skill at school.

The forms of assessment we use in schools have a powerful influence on the kinds of learning that students do, and the kinds of teaching their teachers use. If the good learner is essentially the person plus their resources (and their ability to draw on them), our methods of testing should encourage teachers and students to value and practise capitalising. In today's world, it makes as much sense to sit 15-year-olds down at solitary desks and ask them to display their knowledge and skill as it would to take away David Beckham's football and tell him to perform.

Key points

- Take responsibility for learning
- Plan and organise learning
- Revise along the way
- Monitor and review progress

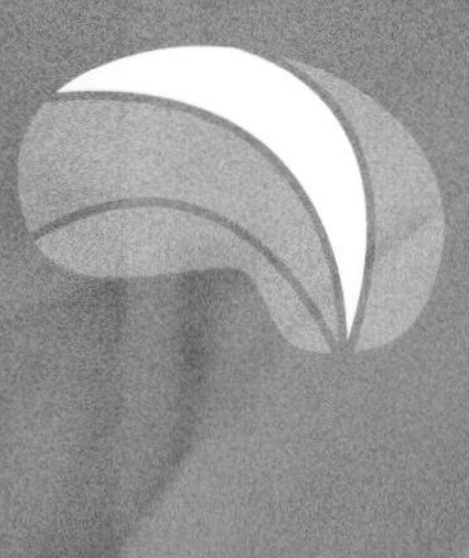

The learning-power mind

Reflectiveness

planning	working learning out in advance
revising	monitoring and adapting along the way
distilling	drawing out the lessons from experience
meta-learning	understanding learning, and yourself as a learner

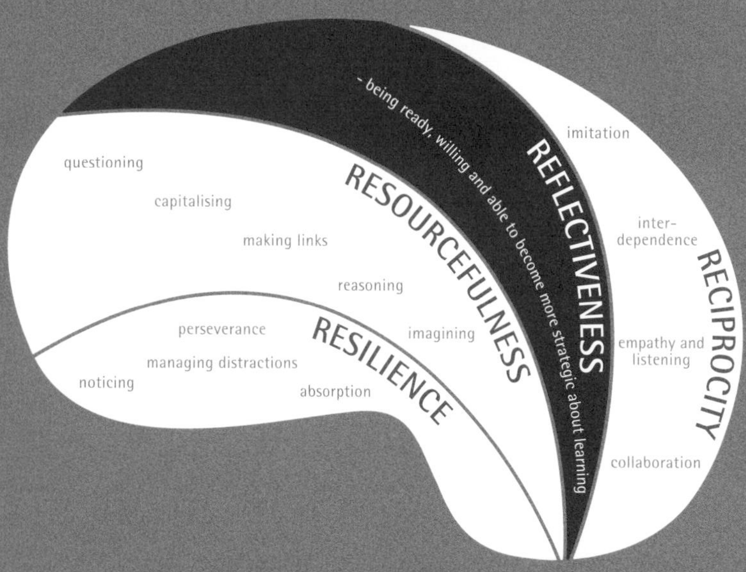

Reflective: ready, willing and able to become more strategic about learning

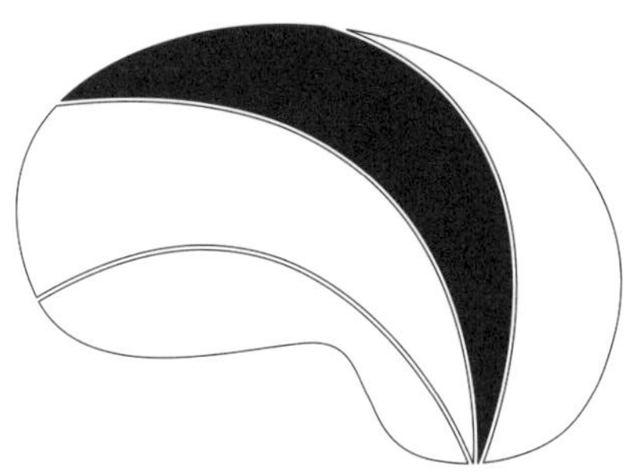

The third aspect of a supple learning-powered mind has to do with self-knowledge and self-awareness. Good learners are intuitive, but they also need to be aware of how their learning is going, and make strategic decisions about it. There are several aspects to reflectiveness, which we call **planning, revising, distilling** and **meta-learning.**

Planning

The first aspect, planning, is the ability to take a strategic overview of your learning, and make sensible decisions. It means:

- taking stock of the problem and the parameters within which you must work
- assessing the available resources, both inner and outer, and deciding which you think are going to be needed
- making an estimate of the time the learning will take, and the competing priorities that may have to be delayed or sacrificed
- imagining a route-map for the learning
- anticipating hurdles or problems that may arise along the way.

Good learners like taking responsibility for planning and organising their learning. They welcome opportunities to decide for themselves when, where, why and how they are going to learn—and to get better at doing so. Research shows, for example, that people who can make a reasonable estimate of how long a task will take are more likely to finish on time, and to do better work.

Revising

The second aspect of reflectiveness is revising. However well prepared learners are, they have to expect the unexpected. So planning has to be accompanied by the readiness to revise as they go along. Good learners are able to change their plans and think on their feet. They are able to be flexible. It may be a good decision to say 'This is turning out to be far harder than I thought, and I'm getting less help than I imagined, and there are other interesting possibilities opening up, so I think I'll cut my losses and quit.' Note that the decision is based on a realistic cost-benefit analysis of the actual situation, not on frustration, pique or a blow to self-esteem.

To be effective at revising, learners need to *monitor* how things are going and periodically *review* where they have got to.

Monitoring is the art of looking over your own shoulder as you're working away at a problem, asking yourself how it's going.

Key points

- Change tack when appropriate
- Mull over experience
- Draw out lessons and generalisations
- Look for new contexts for learning

Five-year-olds can reflect on their learning

Given the chance, and the right kind of encouragement, even children as young as five or six can be reflective about their own learning. Sian, a bright five-year-old, is clearly a better reflector than she is a speller. She wrote in her 'learning log' that she had 'bean wating to No how the Best way to laene is, and the eysistist [easiest]'. With a little prompting from her teacher, Hilary Dyer, she ventured an answer to her own question. 'I think the eest and the best way to laene is not to gese [but to] think.' In her report of this work, Hilary concluded: 'From an early age children are able to engage meaningfully in dialogue about their own learning, and can use frameworks offered by the teacher to access their own intuitive understanding of themselves as learners. This seems to indicate that teachers could now desist from treating the children as passengers in the voyage of their own learning, and [instead] treat young learners as co-pilots.'

RESEARCH TELLS US . . .

Sometimes it's better not to know what you're trying to do

Schools have often been preoccupied with the kind of learning in which you are trying to get to a clearly-defined goal. But not all learning is like that. And sometimes holding on to the 'clear goal', as events unfold, is not the smartest thing to do. A famous study of art students, for example, found that the best pictures are produced by students who refuse to decide what they are trying to achieve until long after they have started painting. They insist on keeping an open mind, and are thus more alive to new, unforeseen possibilities that emerge as the painting progresses. They are continually reflecting not just on how to proceed, but on where they are going, and this enables them to be more creative than their more firm minded fellows.

Reflective . . .

Getting better at monitoring involves cultivating the little voice of self-awareness that keeps the strategic goals in mind, and is ready to change tack if it seems appropriate. A football manager contemplating making a substitution is monitoring, as is a teacher who decides to throw away the lesson plan on the spur of the moment and go with the interesting discussion which is developing. Students can pick up the habit and the skill of this kind of monitoring by being around people—teachers are ideally placed—who are able to model it, and who have learnt how to *learn aloud*, i.e. to externalise the thought processes of the vigilant monitor.

Reviewing means stopping every so often to take stock of progress, and to ensure that any emerging product—an artwork, an essay, a draft business plan—is on track.

Reviewing requires the ability to look at your own work with the critical eye of an editor, and not be afraid of the possibility that some corrections may be needed.

A writer may put a piece of work aside for a while and then come back to look at it afresh. An athlete may sit down and look at the video of her starting technique to see if any adjustments need to be made.

But reviewing is what the low-achieving maths student, for example, is very often unable to do.

Donald Schon called monitoring 'reflection in action', and reviewing 'reflection on action'. Again, modelling and coaching can help develop these abilities.

Distilling

The third aspect of reflectiveness we call distilling (though it includes *bottling* and *transporting* as well). It involves mulling over experience, either alone or in discussion with others, looking for useful lessons and generalisations that can be drawn out and articulated, and which can therefore be consciously applied to new situations. A student teacher may lie in bed ruminating on the day's ups and downs, sifting experiences to see what patterns emerge, and whether any ideas about 'where I am going wrong' and 'how I might do it better' come to mind. A group of school students might get together to chew over a playground incident, looking for things to be wary of in similar situations in the future.

Part of distilling is deliberately looking for new areas or contexts where learning lessons could be applied. It involves a conscious attempt to expand the range of utility of an insight, a concept or a technique. Having learned how to do mind mapping in one context, a student could be encouraged to look for other places where it could usefully be applied, for example. 'I've learnt how to do mind maps in biology, in the context of animal habitats. Could I use them in preparing for a history essay, or in trying to sort out the different ways I go wrong in my algebra?' This is a habit of mind that teachers need to cultivate if they want the skills of their subject to transfer more widely. Unless this process of transfer is given explicit attention, what has been learnt is likely to remain embedded within the subject matter, and its wider relevance will not be perceived.

Key points

- Understand the process of learning
- Know about yourself as a learner
- Articulate how learning works
- Weigh up your learning strengths and weaknesses

A selection of 'reflections'

by a group of 12-year-olds at Northolt High School

Chris Watkins, London Institute of Education

'I'm a great learner when I like the activity I'm concentrating on. If I don't like it I don't listen as much and I am easily distracted.'

'I only really try hard for subjects I'm not good at. I like learning because I want a good job. I like doing practical work because I'm good at it.'

'I have to try something and do it wrong to understand it. I don't like to read instructions.'

'I like to listen to the teacher and try my own ways. I like to work with a friend because they can help you, and I like the TV on or music. The TV has to be not too loud, also slow and smooth music.'

'I learn better in the morning because I am all refreshed.'

RESEARCH TELLS US . . .

'Learning about learning has more impact than study skills. One programme used material from the history curriculum making it the object of reflection; another used generic learning skills materials. The students in the first group developed more advanced conceptions of learning, got better grades on essays and achieved better examination results.'

Chris Watkins, London Institute of Education.

Reflective . . .

This kind of 'chewing the cud' of experience, in order to extract more explicit meaning and direction, is what people sometimes take the whole of 'reflection' to be. But in BLP it is just one aspect of it.

Meta-learning

The fourth aspect of reflectiveness is called meta-learning, and it relies upon a particularly important kind of distilling. It involves drawing out of your learning experience a more general, explicit understanding of the process of learning, and specific knowledge about yourself as a learner. Let's take these two aspects of meta-learning in turn.

There is a wealth of research which shows that good learners know a lot about learning.

They possess a vocabulary for talking about the process of learning itself, and are able to articulate how learning works.

Good readers, even quite young ones, are often able tell you half-a-dozen things they can do when they come across an unfamiliar word: they sound it out, break it down into bits, re-read the previous sentence, read on to see if the meaning becomes clear, look at the picture and think about it, and so on. And so, more generally, for good learners. The more able they are to talk about their learning, the more likely they are to be able to apply their knowledge to new domains too: meta-learning increases generalisation.

And good learners also need an accurate sense of themselves as learners. Being a good learner means being able to take your own strengths and weaknesses into account as you are weighing up a learning challenge, or deciding on a course of 'professional development.' In the business world, it is common now for people to take a job (if they are lucky enough to have a choice) partly on the basis of what they hope to learn from it. To make that decision well, they need not only to be able to plan their learning career, but also to base their decision on a realistic assessment of what they need and are ready to learn. Again, plenty of practice in thinking and talking about oneself as a learner at school is good preparation for the future.

The skills and dispositions of meta-learning can be cultivated simply by a teacher's persistent use of questions such as 'How did you go about finding that out?' or 'How would you go about teaching that to other people?'

Key points

- Balance interactive and solitary learning
- Share and communicate skills and ideas
- Listen to understand
- Be independent in your judgement

RESILIENCE
RESOURCEFULNESS
REFLECTIVENESS
RECIPROCITY

The learning-power mind

Reciprocity

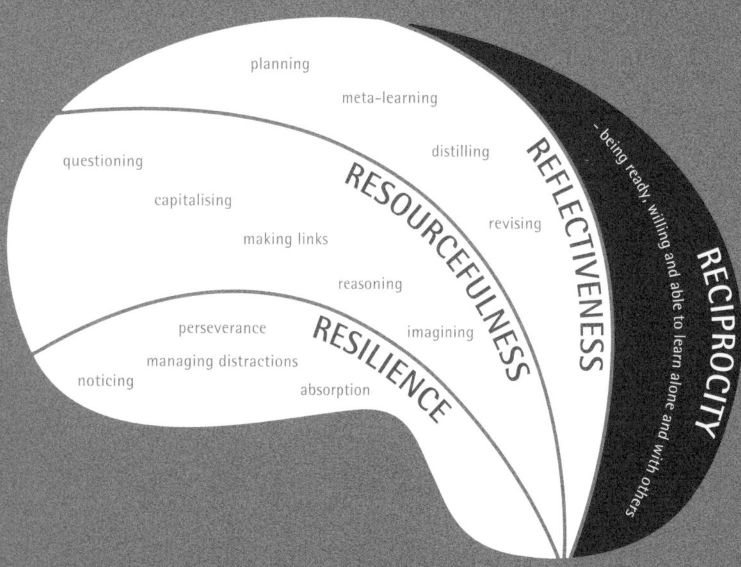

interdependence	balancing self-reliance and sociability
collaboration	the skills of learning with others
empathy and listening	getting inside others' minds
imitation	picking up others' habits and values

Reciprocal: ready, willing and able to learn alone and with others

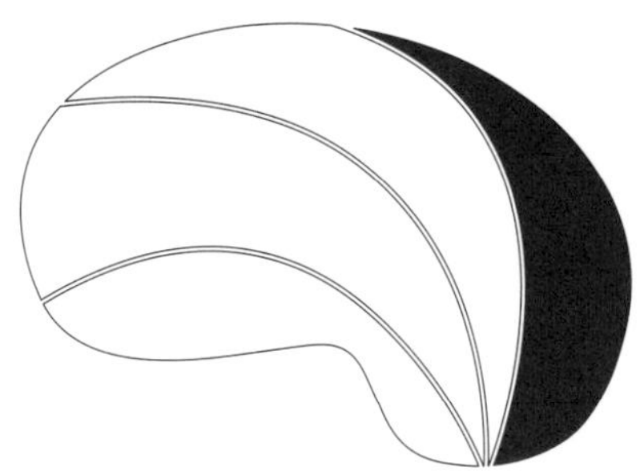

The last aspect of a supple learning-powered mind concerns learners' relationships with other people. Again both skills and inclinations are involved. Sometimes learning has to be a collaborative activity. Team work is the norm in many businesses, and the lone innovator is today the exception rather than the rule.

The ability to listen, take your turn, and understand the viewpoint of someone with whom you do not immediately agree, are all useful for the learner.

Even when collaboration is not required, it often makes good sense to try ideas out on someone else, or know whose brains to pick, and when. We break reciprocity down into four components: **interdependence, collaboration, empathy and listening,** and **imitation.**

Interdependence

Interdependence is not the opposite of collaboration but of *dependency.* Good learners know how to manage the balance between interacting and being solitary in their learning. The balance is often different at different phases of learning. And people differ in how much interaction they need, and at what stages. But however much they interact, good learners are capable of being independent in their judgement and in the extent to which they take control and responsibility for their own learning. They are autonomous even when they are collaborating. Many people talk about the virtues of independent learning, but they often seem to envisage the lone pioneer rather than the balanced person of BLP. The major stimulus to developing inner independence is being given manageable amounts of responsibility for choosing when, where and how to go about learning. This process can begin in the nursery, and continue into the office.

Collaboration

Collaboration involves knowing how to learn with others. It means being able to work as part of a pair or a team, in a situation where no one person is in possession of all parts of the puzzle, and where the sharing of information and ideas is essential. Collaboration means being willing to share, and having the skills of communication to do so effectively. In many primary schools, Circle Time, for example, is already being used as a way of cultivating the requisite attitudes and abilities. Classes can be constituted as a group of research teams, each of which has responsibility for finding out part of the answer to a whole-class project, and then sharing that research with the other teams.

Key points

- Cultivate the habit of listening
- Listen to generate empathy
- Pick up others' ways of thinking and working

The value of discussion

Interviewer: Do you find other students' opinions valuable?

Bill: Yes!

Interviewer: Even if they're wrong?

Bill: Well, plenty of time I'm wrong. The discussion gets everybody involved. I've learnt more this way rather than copying off the board, it stays in your head more, you think about it.

Shane: If you're not understanding something then they [the other students] may understand it better and say it in a different way to what the teacher says . . . They may ask questions you haven't thought of.

from the PEEL Project, Victoria, Australia

'I learned the way a monkey learns: by watching its parents.'

Queen Elizabeth II (allegedly)

RESEARCH TELLS US . . .

Communities of inquiry

Students learn a great deal about all the four Rs, but especially reciprocity, in classrooms that are designed as 'communities of inquiry'. Ann Brown of Harvard University, for example, would set a whole class a juicy topic for a project, and then divide the class in different ways. Sometimes they would think and debate as a whole group. Often they broke into 'research groups', each taking a different aspect of the topic to investigate. Every so often, the class would reconfigure into 'jigsaw groups', comprising one delegate from each of the research teams, which shared problems and progress for the delegates to take back to their research teams. Across a wide range of measures of learning, thinking and communicating, Brown's classrooms show impressive and long-lasting gains. Students learn more, but more importantly, they are building up their learning power.

Reciprocal . . .

Empathy and listening

Empathy and listening are core skills of reciprocity. We bracket them together because listening is the main medium through which empathy is generated and communicated. Students can quite readily be coached in the art of being a good listener, and can be given games and exercises that help them develop the ability to hear what someone else has said and, if necessary, play it back to them. Teachers sometimes complain that students will not listen, either to them or to each other; but the habit of listening can be cultivated in most classes inside a term. The most powerful way to do this is for the teachers to model good listening.

There is some suggestion that people who suffer from autism lack the ability to see the world through other people's eyes. And it is also possible that many bullies have failed to develop the ability to read other people's emotional signals. But for the vast majority of students, empathy develops with a little encouragement.

Imitation

Finally, imitation involves the disposition to pick up other people's ways of thinking, learning, working and evaluating simply through taking part in joint activity with them, and seeing and hearing how they go about things. The great Russian psychologist Lev Vygotsky pointed out how much of our mentality—the ways we interpret the world, and think and learn about it—we have internalised from the significant others with whom we have worked, played or solved problems. Just as Darren was soaking up other people's skill on the dancefloor, so

We absorb the mental strategies and habits of those we admire and trust.

Scientists have suggested that this semi-conscious mode of cultural transmission may play a more important role in human development than any amount of deliberate instruction.

Key points

- Pay attention in a variety of ways
- Develop a toolkit of learning attributes
- Use a range of reflective techniques

RESILIENCE

RESOURCEFULNESS

REFLECTIVENESS

RECIPROCITY

The learning-power mind

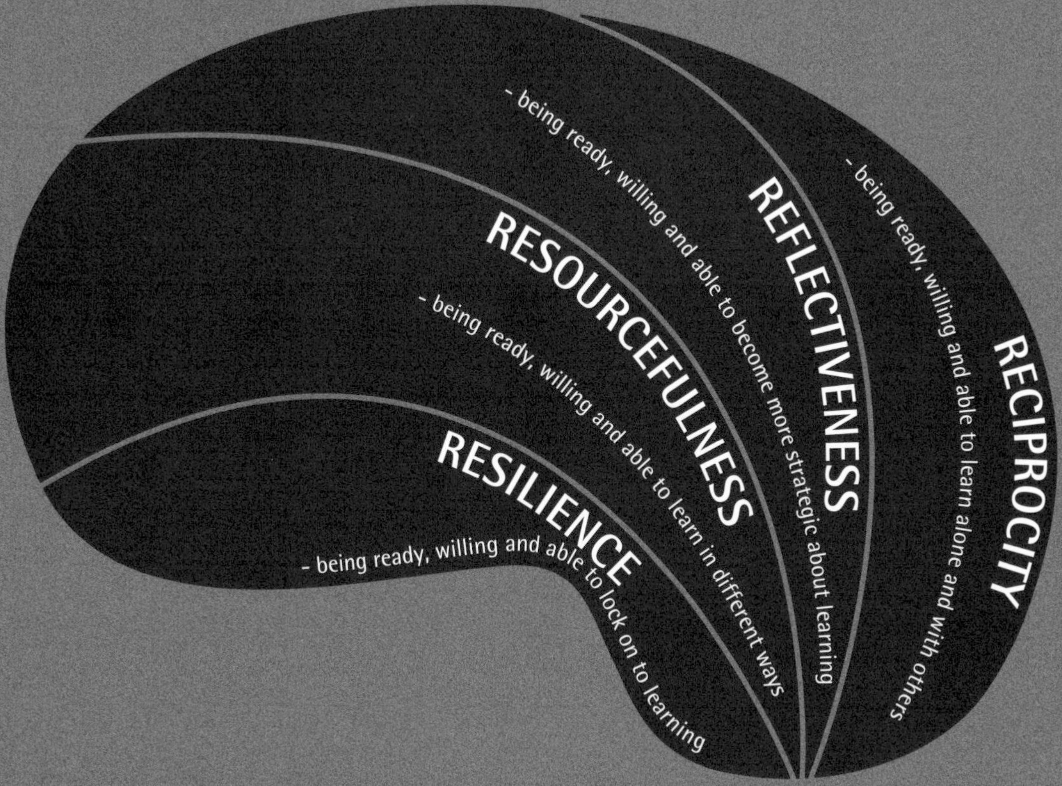

RESILIENCE - being ready, willing and able to lock on to learning

RESOURCEFULNESS - being ready, willing and able to learn in different ways

REFLECTIVENESS - being ready, willing and able to become more strategic about learning

RECIPROCITY - being ready, willing and able to learn alone and with others

The story so far

So far we have drawn a sketch map of the attributes of effective real-life learners, spiced with just a few hints about how these qualities and capabilities can be cultivated.

Good learners have what we called resilience: they are able to 'lock on' to learning, to pay attention to what is going on around them, in a variety of ways.

And they can maintain and restore their attention in the face of distractions and interruptions. They especially need to be able to tolerate the feelings of learning—apprehension, frustration and confusion—and the possibility of making mistakes, without getting upset and breaking contact with their learning too soon, or for too long.

Good learners use a varied toolkit of learning methods and attitudes to make them resourceful.

They are comfortable with the uncertainty that lies behind a questioning attitude, and they enjoy exploring and investigating. They are on the look-out for all kinds of links between what they are studying or exploring and what they know already—intellectual, personal and practical. They know how and when to use their imagination, and are willing to make use both of mental rehearsal of specific skills and situations, and to indulge, from time to time, in the more subtle and receptive art of reverie, which is the incubator of creativity. They can think systematically, analytically and logically when the time is right, and move fluidly between different modes of thinking to suit the learning task at hand. They are good at spotting, uncovering or fabricating all kinds of external aids and resources to help support learning, and off-load some of the cognitive effort onto smart machines like filing cabinets, spreadsheets and the internet.

Good learners are reflective in a range of different ways.

They can plan their learning sometimes, though sometimes they just let it happen without too much supervision. Being able to make good strategic decisions about learning methods and learning career is important. Good learners have the self-awareness to monitor their learning, and change course when circumstances change. They stop and take stock of their progress, and reflect on their products in a realistic and sometimes critical way. They think about what they are learning that might be useful in different settings, and explore in their minds how to disembed their knowledge from specific contexts, to increase its range and power. They know how to think and talk about learning, and are comfortable talking with others about the learning process. And they apply that knowledge to themselves, to develop an accurate and flexible image of themselves as developing learners.

Key points

- Have a sense of independent judgement
- Join the give and take of collaborative learning
- Learn from other people
- Test your own ideas about learning

Empathy

'Empathy means entering the private perceptual world of the other and becoming thoroughly at home in it. It means temporarily living in his/her life, moving about in it delicately without making judgements . . . To be with another in this way means that for the time being you lay aside the views and values you hold for yourself in order to enter another's world without prejudice.'

Carl Rogers, founder of client centered psychotherapy.

RESEARCH TELLS US . . .

Built to imitate

Neuroscientists have recently discovered that there are neurones in the brain that are specially designed for imitation. Mostly, each neuron has just one particular kind of event that gets it excited. Everything else leaves it cold. But 'mirror neurons' fire off either when we perform a particular action ourselves, or when we see someone else do it. It's as if we have a built-in predisposition to do what those around us are doing. Maybe that's why yawning is so contagious. But it also means that we are designed to pick up the learning habits of those around us too. That's why teachers need to be models of good learning. And why it is a good idea to learn with other people who bring different skills and perspectives to bear: those will gradually rub off on you.

The story so far . . .

And finally,

Good learners balance their relationships with other people, being willing to be interdependent, without becoming either too dependent on others for support or feedback, or too aloof and unwilling to take criticism or to work as part of a team.

They have a sense of independent judgement, and also the skills to share ideas and join in the give and take of a collaborative learning venture. In particular they can understand and respect the worldviews and positions of people different from themselves, even positions which they do not immediately agree with or find congenial. They can listen carefully to what others are saying, and co-ordinate their responses with the thrust of the conversation. And they are willing to learn from the way other people go about learning and problem-solving, picking up ways of thinking and perceiving as they work together side-by-side.

Some pitfalls

One thing is for sure: being a good learner is not a matter of being 'bright'. It's not to do with the amount of 'brains' you were born with. The old idea that **Achievement = Ability + Effort** is just plain wrong. People with high IQs or good degrees are not always good learners. They may know a lot, and they may have acquired certain rather specialised learning skills, but that doesn't guarantee they will be all-round resilient, resourceful, reflective or reciprocal. In fact high achievers can sometimes be very conservative learners—more frightened of getting it wrong than a baby. We all know clever people who can't see beyond the end of their nose.

In fact, being a good learner can't be boiled down to any small set of concepts or simple tricks or remedies. Einstein said 'we should make things as simple as possible—but not more so'. And the effective mind is like a well-balanced orchestra, not a list of bullet points. So beware of little flow diagrams and check-lists that purport to tell you the whole truth. They may be a very good place to start thinking about learning—but they are an awful place to stop. Good learners test ideas about learning for themselves—even the four Rs!

We now have a reasonably comprehensive map of what the effective learner thinks, feels, believes, values and does. But the key questions are:

- Is it a good idea to try to build young people's learning power? If so,
- Is it any of education's business to do it? And if so,
- Can these habits and qualities be cultivated—especially in 'ordinary' schools?

These are the questions to which we now turn.

Section 2a
Education for the future

What is education for?

This section explains why BLP is needed in the context of the demands of twenty-first century life. Many of young people's stresses and insecurities stem from the fact that they don't feel equal to those demands. We take a look at some of those demands, and how education could do more to prepare young people for a learning life.

What is education for?

At root, education is what societies provide for their young people to help them get ready to make the most of the world they are going to find themselves in. We want them to be able to make a living in a way that is fulfilling, enjoyable and responsible. We want them to be able to use their leisure productively: to have fun in a way that does not harm other people or the common resources of locality or planet. We want them to be able to make successful relationships, to be good parents, to be capable of being (and disposed to be) loving and kind.

We would like them to be naturally respectful of people of different beliefs, faiths and persuasions, especially those who are less fortunate. We would like them to feel able to take part in the public life of their community and nation. We would like them to have clear values and principles, and to live by them. We want them to live, as much as they can, without fear or insecurity. We would like them to be happy.

Different people and different societies might express their aspirations for the next generation in different terms, but all education rests on some such statements of hope.

The attitudes, beliefs and capacities young people will need in order to achieve those goals depend crucially on what their world is going to be like. And the education they will need therefore depends on the accuracy with which the current generation, the designers and providers of education, anticipate what the major challenges and opportunities of the future are going to be. It is no use providing education that prepares young people, however effectively, for a world that they are not going to meet, perhaps one that no longer exists.

In stable times, where the culture is relatively homogeneous and the demands of the future relatively predictable, education can provide young people with the knowledge, skills, and ways of thinking that *we* know *they* are going to need. It is a truism that we do not live in such times: a truism because it is so obviously true.

For the vast majority of young people on the planet (and many of their parents), the world is confusing, complicated and rapidly changing—and likely to get more so over their lifetime.

Most people agree that the only thing we can say with any confidence about the year 2025 is that there is not much we can say about it with any confidence.

In this situation, education has to take a step back. Of course we want to give young people the knowledge and attitudes we value: the trouble is, most societies are now a jumble of different we's. Young people are subject to a welter of conflicting advice and images about what matters, and how to be. It's as if they were standing in the middle of a circle of street-lights, each casting their shadow in a different direction. In a world like this, the only sensible role for education is to get them ready, as much as it can, to cope well with complexity, uncertainty and ambiguity—and to handle the high level of responsibility for crafting their own version of a satisfying life that this challenge entails.

The way the world is going

It does not take an astrologer to know the way the world is going. Mobile phones, e-mail, satellite TV and video games, the internet, cheap international air travel . . . a host of technological innovations have changed the face of work, life and leisure in dozens of ways. Millions of people in the UK work at least part of the time from home. Many of them do daily business with people they have never met. Instead of a 'steady job', people are getting used to being employed for the life of a project: having to adapt quickly to the particular languages and worldviews of team members from diverse professional and cultural backgrounds, and then move on. Microelectronics companies come and go, chasing the best costs-to-skills ratios around the globe, leaving a legacy of deepened insecurity, middle as well as traditionally working class, in their wake. Business people look for security to their financial bonuses, pension funds and their fattening c.v., not to company loyalty.

The traditional heavy industries, and the community life which they supported, are things of the past. The gap between those consultants and 'knowledge workers' who are doing well out of globalisation, and the millions at the poor end of the service industries, packed into call centres, forced to smile on the minimum wage, is widening. As Doug Ross, Assistant Secretary for Employment and Training in the US Department of Labor told an international conference a few years ago, 'the new poor and marginal in the societies of the developed world will be those who cannot or will not engage in lifelong learning.'

These societies have been less clear about what to do about it. They know that

lifelong learning and the learning society cannot boil down to lifelong consumption of professional development and accredited courses.

Yet the idea that schools could—and should—be systematically preparing young people to thrive under the stressful conditions they will increasingly meet is only now catching on.

> *'All education springs from images of the future and all education creates images of the future. Thus all education, whether so intended or not, is a preparation for the future. Unless we understand the future for which we are preparing we do tragic damage to those we teach.'*
>
> Alvin Toffler, *Learning for Tomorrow*

A sense of identity

The world generates exciting opportunities for those well placed to pursue them, and a form of insecurity that is existential as much as vocational or financial, in many others. The questions 'Who am I?' and 'What matters?' used to be answered for youngsters by the community, the region, the family, or the religion they were born into. Now, the majority of UK 11- to 25-year-olds feel as if they belong more to their friendship group than they do even to their families. As they choose their friends, so they implicitly choose how to answer the big questions of identity and values for themselves. Who I am is a Man. U. fan, or Jayne's best friend. What matters more than

What is education for?

anything is that Gareth wins *Pop Idol* talent show, or that Ramesh loves me.

It is not too fanciful to see, behind the youth culture of raves and drugs, sport and celebrity, the rise of teenage pregnancy and fundamentalism, the shadow of insecurity: the feeling of not being able to get a grip on the miasma of choices and opportunities that swirls around them, many of them. No wonder so many young people clutch at the first kind boy or girl, the first shallow ideology, that comes along. It's not so much that many young people live in poverty, though they do, as that they do not know where to turn for direction and value. In such a state, algebra and parts of speech can seem a little beside the point.

The very process of choosing can offer a sense of identity. It can give a feeling of being in charge to weigh up pros and cons and make decisions and selections. Perhaps that's why shopping is such a popular activity. But today's young people have the opportunity, and often the responsibility, to make more fundamental life choices than a pair of jeans—much more than many of their grandparents ever had. You can choose what country you are going to live in. Many people are making conscious choices about their level of economic activity, often deciding to 'down-shift' and earn less, in the belief that they will be happier. You can choose your religion. You can choose to have children or not; to be single; to be gay. Surgery allows you to change your body shape and even your gender if you want to. Many young people have deliberately changed the speech accent they grew up with in order to fit in with a different circle or culture.

The question is: What does it take to make good use of all this freedom and opportunity?

Not all young people are adrift in this sea of complexity and choice, though there are many statistics to support the general picture. But even youngsters well rooted in stable families and communities cannot but be aware of the general insecurity in the air. After interviewing 3,500 11- to 25-year-olds about their views on work, school and the future, the 1997 Industrial Society report *Speaking Up, Speaking Out* concluded that 'Most [young people] fear that their world will generally become more challenging, and some have a bleak view of future opportunities and trends . . . Their lives are riddled with insecurity . . . Schools are seen as failing to equip young people with the ability to learn for life rather than for exams.'

That last sentence is the key. Remember this is the voice of today's youth (not some sociological theory). They are telling us that they are floundering, and that we are not teaching them how to swim. That is why they turn off from school, and focus instead on friends, fashion, fitness and escapism of various kinds. They are not intrinsically lazy or bolshy or lacking ability: they are disappointed in our reactions to their predicament, and flailing about.

In the face of these patent cries for help, how are education systems responding? And are these responses hitting the spot? That is what we shall review briefly in the next section.

Section 2b

Education for the future

Schools in reform: how far have we got?

This section reviews the flurry of reforms that are being tried out in education systems worldwide. It argues that most attempts to tinker with forms of curriculum, management and assessment miss the point. Young people want and need to learn how to learn. The section will help you understand why so many expensive initiatives seem to produce so little real change.

How far have we got?

People both inside and outside education are eager to know if there is anywhere in the world that has got the right education system to meet the conflicting demands of the twenty-first century. The evidence doesn't seem very positive. Around 15% of school leavers in the UK still struggle with basic literacy and numeracy while far too many leave school with no relevant qualifications at all. And are those who have been successful at school any more equipped to be participating learners? Not according to the university lecturers who complain that students are ill-prepared to manage their own learning effectively. Meanwhile employers cry out for job applicants—including graduates—who are able to exercise initiative and take greater personal responsibility. A succession of surveys reveals that too many students are bored by their lessons and can't see the point in what they learn in school. The knock-on effect is that teachers' lives become more difficult; their stress levels continue to rise and they become less able to respond creatively to their pupils' needs. If recruitment and retention of teachers is a problem at the beginning of the twenty-first century, it will become more so as the large numbers of middle-aged teachers reach retirement age. Dispirited teachers find it hard to generate exciting and relevant lessons. Young people disengage from school and their parents are punished for letting their children play truant.

Various cures

Everyone knows that this vicious circle must be broken. Governments throughout the world generate their own pet diagnoses and preferred cures. As yet, there is no blueprint that assures success. Some, such as the UK, believe that teachers have had too much autonomy and that tighter specifications of what and how they teach, and how they assess their pupils, will improve standards. So, a National Curriculum is devised, contested and adjusted; students are subjected to age-related tests and the results are anxiously compared with those from other countries. Meanwhile some of these other countries, Finland for example, are equally convinced that the solution lies in less central control, and are busy devolving responsibility and creativity to individual schools and teachers.

Some governments, such as those in the UK, think that the 'progressive' teaching methods of the 1970s are to blame for 'low standards', and insist on a 'back to basics' approach to teaching and learning. 'What's wrong with spoon-feeding' they ask, 'if spoon-feeding raises levels of literacy and numeracy?' Some hark back nostalgically to days of firmer discipline where there was greater deference for authority. Others, such as Singapore, are just as worried that their 'traditional' teaching methods have been producing generations of young people who are good at mental arithmetic but cannot think for themselves. They are insisting that their teachers adopt the kinds of open and creative approaches to education, which UK governments have tried so hard to eradicate.

Some see the solution in the way schools are financed and managed. Perhaps everyone would be galvanised into producing better results if schools were run more like businesses, or even managed by people with a good track record of running profitable commercial concerns?

If so, headteachers need to be equipped with the unfamiliar skills of budgeting and marketing, with governors exercising greater local control over how a school raises and spends its money. Others baulk at the potential for the worst excesses of commercialism—companies offering free video and computer equipment to schools on condition that students spend so many minutes an hour watching advertisements for trainers and fast food.

Some people pin their hopes for the revitalisation of education on 'information and communication technology'. They think that the provision of expensive machines throughout our schools will liberate children from mundane, boring lessons, revitalise their learning and unleash their imaginations.

On the other hand, there are those who say that many students are doing more complicated, challenging and imaginative things on the PC in their bedroom than they would ever do in school; that machines can create dependency just as much as liberation; and that Bill Gates is only able to be a philanthropist because he is first and foremost an astute and ruthless businessman.

What has changed?

Across the world there is an expanding wreckers' yard full of those educational initiatives that never quite fulfilled their promise; if they didn't work why should we be anything but wary and sceptical about any new models for reform? City Technology Colleges, Education Action Zones, specialist schools, Beacon schools, inclusion projects, regeneration initiatives—dozens of innovations have come and gone over the last 20 years in the UK, and yet we are left with the same concerns and dissatisfactions. It may be time to look more closely at the wine of good learning rather than concentrating on creating new bottles in which to put the same old wine.

The problem is that, for all this flurry of activity and innovation, the experience of many young people in schools and classrooms has not changed dramatically in generations. The emphasis has remained firmly on the content to be learnt rather than the processes of learning.

Despite all the movement in education, we have still been working with a nineteenth-century set of assumptions.

We still assume that it is teachers' central task to transmit bodies of knowledge, skill and understanding. We still think it is valid to use exams like dipsticks, to check the level of knowledge in pupils' minds, as if minds were sumps with finite capacities. We still think that students' achievements can be simply ascribed to some hypothetical general-purpose 'ability' enhanced with a touch of added 'effort'. We still think that all children learn in the same way, differing only in their speed.

How far have we got?

'Educators of the mid-nineteenth century explicitly borrowed their new designs [for schools] from the factory-builders they admired . . . The result of this machine-age thinking was a model of school separate from daily life, governed in an authoritarian manner, oriented above all else to producing a standardized product, the labor input needed for the rapidly growing industrial-age workplace . . . Those who did not learn at the speed of the assembly line either fell off or were forced to struggle continually to keep pace: they were labelled "slow" or, in today's more fashionable jargon, "learning disabled" . . . Finally, the assembly-line model tacitly identified students as the product rather than the creators of learning, passive objects being shaped by an educational process beyond their influence.'

Peter Senge, *Schools That Learn*

Instead, we need reform that is based on a different set of core ideas. They are the realisations that:

- students can learn to learn more effectively
- many of their difficulties are actually opportunities to strengthen their learning power
- strengthening learning power is what education for the twenty-first century should centrally be about

None of these mean throwing out or watering down the content, just dealing with it in a slightly different way.

Section 2c

Education for the future

Reform for the future

This section focuses on some of the reforms that are successfully helping young people develop their learning power. We concentrate here on those that are practical and effective and show how BLP fits in with other similar kinds of reforms worldwide.

Reform for the future

Though some current reforms are doomed to be expensive and time-consuming failures, there are many chinks of light. Building learning power draws on dozens of examples from around the world of how schools can enhance students' learning power, and get better results, at the same time. There is a gathering body of both theory and practice which shows that the stale old opposition between 'traditional' and 'progressive'—learning for exams vs. learning for life—can be successfully transcended. It is possible, in regular schools with regular students, to do both.

- The Golden Key schools in Russia are based in Vygotsky's principles of social learning and take children between the ages of 4 and 16 years. They achieve high standards on national tests, yet their main emphases are on the development of imagination, and on enabling children of different ages to learn how to learn from each other.
- Ann Brown's Communities of Inquiry in Cambridge, Massachusetts—as we have seen (page 38)—develop even young students' powers of collaboration and communication, and their skills as researchers. Not surprisingly, they enjoy learning more and become better at it.
- The Project for the Enhancement of Effective Learning (PEEL) in Australia shows that students' performance in school improves as they learn to notice and talk about their own learning.
- At the York School in Toronto, as children in the second grade are encouraged to ask and research their own questions in science, so the quality of both their questioning and their understanding improves.
- And at Christ Church Primary School in Wiltshire, England, 11-year-olds learn a variety of strategies for 'unsticking' themselves when they don't know what to do—and their Key Stage 2 SATs results have rocketed.

Here are the main characteristics of the BLP approach.

- **Practical.** BLP is above all a practical approach. It contains dozens of ideas that can be tried out in almost any school. It does not depend on teachers who have outstanding reserves of energy or charisma, or students who are especially biddable or 'bright'. Some other approaches have been long on good intentions but short on smart things to do; some only work under especially favourable conditions. In BLP, we start small and build; not fly high and crash.
- **Enjoyable.** BLP aims to makes both learning and teaching more enjoyable. Students who become more interested and confident in their developing learning power are less likely to drift off task when they find learning difficult. BLP is not a cure-all for every difficulty, and it will not immediately engage the interest of the most disaffected students. But the majority of young people quickly grasp the idea of learning to learn, and find it relevant to their own lives and concerns. Most teachers find that, as their students become more resilient, resourceful, reflective and reciprocal, so the amount of chivvying and firefighting they have to do decreases.
- **Sound.** BLP is based on an extensive body of research. The new sciences of brain and mind are revealing just how learnable

learning is—and are casting increasing doubt on the old idea that a person's learning is largely determined by some kind of fixed reservoir of general-purpose ability or intelligence. Where some other approaches to learning-to-learn have based themselves on rather dubious ideas of 'brain-friendly learning', BLP draws on solid evidence.

- Comprehensive. The four Rs give a coherent overview of what it takes to be a good learner. Some other approaches highlight just a few aspects of learning to learn and neglect the others. They might focus on self-esteem, for example, and ignore the development of imagination. Or they might aim to cultivate the ability to plan learning in a strategic and systematic way, and underestimate the importance of quiet attentiveness or playing with possibilities. Some emphasise the individual and ignore collaboration and empathy.
- Forward-looking. BLP has two goals: to raise standards (in conventional terms), and to give young people a flying start on a learning life. We think that knowledge and qualifications are important, but they are not enough. We want young people to develop qualities and habits of mind in school that will stand them in good stead outside of school, for the rest of their lives. BLP goes beyond improving educational attainment and achievement. Its aims are more ambitious (without becoming unrealistic or idealistic).
- Inclusive. The scientific foundations of BLP show that it is not something that is only suitable for the gifted and talented: it is for everyone. Everyone can get better at learning. Some people will always achieve more in some areas of life than others, but that does not mean that it is a waste of time developing your learning power. (I am never going to have the strength of Sir Steve Redgrave or the speed of Linford Christie, but that does not mean that there is no point in my going to the gym.) Not everyone is cut out to be academic, but we are all built to learn—and to get better at it.
- Holistic. BLP understands that learning depends on all aspects of a person's psychology: not just their cognitive skills and strategies, but their attitudes, values, beliefs and emotions. That is why the development of learning power goes beyond 'study skills' and affects the whole culture of the classroom, and indeed the overall climate of a school. It reinforces the importance of the key skills of problem solving, working with others, and improving learning and performance. BLP develops *dispositions to learn*, as well as learning capabilities.
- Flexible. Learning is a multifarious business. There is no one best way of learning: it depends on what you are learning and what the context is. Sometimes you need to be methodical, sometimes opportunistic; sometimes quick and incisive, and sometimes slow and contemplative. Professor Robert Sternberg of Yale University, one of the foremost authorities on intelligence, says:

> *'The essence of intelligence would seem to be in knowing when to act quickly and when to think and act slowly.'*

BLP goes beyond accelerated learning, and teaching thinking skills, to cultivate a more general suppleness of mind that enables

Reform for the future . . .

young people to be good all-round learners. Rather than identifying students' dominant 'learning style' or 'multiple intelligence profile', and then encouraging them to play to their (existing) strength, BLP invites them steadily to broaden their portfolio of learning styles, methods and approaches. Instead of cementing students' belief in themselves as a certain type of learner, BLP works on developing the ability to learn in different ways.

- Lasting. BLP is cumulative, and aims to develop learning power in a way that lasts and spreads. The goal is to send out into the world young people to whom learning is second nature: who naturally manifest the four Rs whenever and wherever they might be appropriate. These young people will be able to use their 'learning muscles' both in formal learning situations and in every aspect of their daily lives. Many concentrated attempts to teach thinking skills, for example, show (sometimes impressive) short-term gains that have fizzled out three months later. In a school that has fully embraced BLP, learning-to-learn grows year by year.
- Systematic. BLP systematically develops the habits of learning. So it is not to be confused with approaches that rest on a more romantic, laisser-faire or child-centred philosophy. Some of these almost seem to consider it an insult to the child's spirit to try to influence his or her growth. Although BLP does indeed value creativity, imagination and independence of mind, it places equal emphasis on hard, rational thinking and persistent effort. This is not a matter of ideology, but of the practical needs of the next generation.
- Transparent. One of the strengths of BLP is the direct involvement of students in exploring learning-to-learn for themselves, and in generating strategies for improving their own learning. BLP shifts responsibility for learning to learn from the teacher to the learner. Traditionally teachers have taken most of the responsibility for designing and directing learning-to-learn activities. They created the conditions (of 'high challenge, low threat', for example) under which students were supposed to work best. Students were the recipients of ideas and activities which they had not had any active role in designing or investigating. In BLP, teachers share ideas and intentions about learning to learn with their students.
- Creative. BLP is owned and developed jointly by teachers and students. Although the approach offers a wealth of information and practical possibilities, these are designed to stimulate a more creative engagement by both teachers and students. Instead of the teachers bringing definitive knowledge about learning, usually gleaned from an 'expert' trainer, authority or manual, they open up questions, suggest possibilities, and invite their students to become researchers into learning to learn for themselves. It is essential to the approach that all its ideas are developed critically, in unpredictable ways, by different classes and schools. BLP fails if its ideas are applied mechanically or mindlessly.
- Communal. Finally, BLP aims to make classes and schools not just learning communities, but *learning-about-learning communities*. Generating and elaborating ideas about how to learn better becomes a

collective enterprise, to which all members of a school community—parents and learning support assistants, as well as teachers and students—can contribute. Learning to learn evolves from being purely an individual matter, and extends beyond the classroom into the life of the school as a whole. BLP develops knowledge and expertise about learning that is publicly displayed, discussed and celebrated.

Beyond fashion

Despite all the current rhetoric about lifelong learning and the learning society, there is no denying that BLP looks, in some ways, deeply unfashionable. For example, it is a little sceptical about the current obsessions with speed and ICT.

Some of the best learning is slow, and the idea that a slow learner is necessarily less intelligent than someone who always has a fast, fluent answer to every question is itself an unintelligent point of view.

Clever machines certainly aid some kinds of learning, but it is our view that they will never replace the collaborative and contagious learning that lies at the heart of learning to learn.

The mastery of certain bodies of knowledge is important: but from the BLP perspective, arguments about what to teach hinge less on what is intrinsically valuable knowledge, than on the extent to which any topic affords opportunities for learning how to learn. Just as the equipment in a gym is there not to be studied but to be used (in the service of building strength and fitness), so is the content of the curriculum. Looked at in this light, every topic would need to defend its place in the curriculum on the grounds that it offers a suitably engaging and challenging 'work-out' for the developing learner.

In one sense BLP is not just unfashionable, but decidedly old-fashioned. It is concerned with the development of *character.* In the old days, the key qualities that education sought to develop were leadership and erudition for the few, and compliance and reliability for the many. Now the world has changed, and everyone—for personal as well as vocational reasons—needs the qualities of effective real-life learners which we have been talking about. The valued characteristics are different, but the idea that education is about more than qualifications remains central.

People who blanch at this idea need to remember that education *always* encourages the development of certain traits, whether it is acknowledged or not. A spoon-fed curriculum with multiple-choice exams encourages the habit of accurate retention and the attitude of dependency, and discourages questioning and imagination. A laisser-faire 'progressive' education values and encourages independence and creativity, but does not necessarily invite disciplined study and persistence. Implicitly or explicitly, education always cultivates a particular set of characteristics. Recognising this, BLP seeks deliberately to cultivate those qualities of mind and spirit that seem most relevant to life in the twenty-first century.

Section 3a

Building learning power in practice

Meet Rita and Rob: learning power teachers

In this section, you will meet two of Darren and Katie's teachers: Rita Salbiah, the Year 6 teacher at Beckley Road Primary School who taught Darren last year; and Rob George, one of Katie's current lecturers on her course in Sports Centre Management at Paneham College. We see how Rita is preparing for her new batch of students, in a school that is committed to the BLP approach. And we see how Rob tries to encourage Katie's developing learning skills and interests. Together, they will give you an idea of how BLP teachers think and work.

informing

nudging

discussing

reminding

replying

tracking

selecting

framing

questioning

curiosity

target setting

reacting

learning aloud

sharing

Meet Rita and Bob: learning power teachers

Like Darren, Rita Salbiah, his old Year 6 teacher at Beckley Road Primary School, has a big day tomorrow: the start of a new school year, and another mixed bag of 10-year-olds to welcome to the mind gym (which is what she calls her classroom now). She knows that the first week of term will be crucial, and—again like Darren—she is quietly running through in her mind the most important things that she wants to set in place.

First, she will get the children to make links back to what they were doing last year with Diana Rowe. Di, she knows, likes to get her students to think of themselves as 'learning detectives', and has lots of posters about famous sleuths (which she had made), and others that summarise the children's own ideas about what being a good detective entails. She had copied a few of these to make the children feel at home, and to help them get a sense of continuity between the years.

Then she will get them to recall some of their own learning power highs and lows from the previous year, and to think about which areas of their 'learning power jigsaw puzzle' they want to work on in the first half term. Back in Year 1 the children had started with a simple four-piece jigsaw—one for each of the four Rs—which their teacher helped them to build up. By the time they got to Year 5, their jigsaws were much more detailed and comprehensive, covering all the subdivisions of the four Rs like **collaboration**, **making links** and **being absorbed**, and the students had learned to monitor their own progress, and to explain to the teacher why they thought they deserved a new piece for their developing puzzle. In Year 6, they were now ready to discover new areas of the 'learning power map' for themselves, and to decide their own criteria and set their own targets.

She will get them to talk in threes about how they tackled various challenges and uncertainties over the summer, and how they are different now from when they were four or five. This will be her way in to preparing them for their role as 'learning buddies' to the new kids in Reception. The school has decided to pair each of the little ones with a Year 6 to help them get the hang of the four Rs, and Rita has thought long and hard about how best to prepare her sophisticated 10-year-olds for this responsibility. She definitely wants them to see it as a learning challenge for themselves—What are they going to need to learn?—as well as of value to their younger partners. She is going to risk trying a role-play (though Di has said that her attempts at role-play didn't go very well with this group for some reason). She has also decided that she will need to find 20 minutes or so every week for a while to talk with her class about how it is going, and what problems they are encountering. She will get the class to keep a record of their ups and downs so they can create a 'coaching manual' for the next cohort of learning buddies. She is pretty sure that doing this will help them crystallise the learning lessons out of their own experience.

Rita is also determined to take the risk of revealing more of her own learning exploits—warts and all. She was inspired last year by the corner of the classroom in which Di—trained as a biologist—carried out her own experiments on trying to create hybrid plants, explaining

Learning power teachers . . .

to the children what she was doing, recording her failures, and asking for their suggestions. Since her English degree, Rita has kept up her own poetry writing, and has even had a couple published. Over the summer she kept the contents of her waste-paper basket, and has made a display of all the scrunched-up drafts of a long poem she is working on. She still hasn't got it right, but wants to try talking to her class about the progress she has made, and all the various feelings along the way. She has an idea (sparked by an old advertisement) for an exercise in which she might get them to recreate imaginatively (and hopefully humorously) earlier drafts of some famous poems. (Did 'I wandered lonely as a cloud' start out as 'I walked about a bit by myself' perhaps?)

Rita has primed the classroom assistants she will be working most closely with—Lorraine and Bill—to discuss some of their own learning with the class. Lorraine has just done her first scuba dive in the sea (after weeks of practising in the local pool), and is going to talk about the fear and the excitement. Bill is a corporal in the Territorial Army and a new grandfather: he'll talk about both learning experiences. Neither of them is at all used to public speaking, and both were rather unnerved by the prospect of talking about themselves to an audience even of children. But they have been included all the way along the line in discussions of the school's BLP approach, and can see the point of revealing their own learning. They can also see the point of modelling 'adults nervously trying something new' for the students. They'll give it a go.

Two miles down the road, and three weeks later, Rob George, lecturer in leisure studies at Paneham College, is marking a pile of first-year essays on exercise and stress. He has just read six that have faithfully paraphrased the course text, and is getting very bored. But this one is different: it's not about how exercise relieves stress, but about how stress causes people to change their attitudes to exercise. Some people, the author suggests, become obsessional joggers or squash players when they are stressed—and they exercise in a stressed way, always pushing themselves, setting targets and competing fiercely. Others turn into couch potatoes. What's the difference? There are some ideas about 'type A and type B personalities'—which is certainly not in the course—and thoughts about body-image, self-perception and gender. The style is rather rough, but it's interesting. Rob is surprised to see it's by Katie Kowalski. Well, well. He writes very encouraging comments at the end, suggesting that she might reflect on how she had come to develop these ideas, and how she might develop them. 'Could we use the whole class to explore these ideas further?' he asks, 'And how could we do it? Questionnaires? Interviews? A whole-class discussion? Let me know if you'd like to pursue this.' Rob wants to be positive but without being pressurising: he knows that not all seeds of good ideas are ripe for development at once.

For a break from marking, Rob decides to tee up some videos. Later on in the term, he is going to weave in to his classes some of the information he has been collecting about learning and the brain. He has videos of a TV series about the neurological basis of learning, and wants to focus on how learning is affected by nutrition. He'll get the students to keep a diary of their own diet, and any food supplements they might take, and see if they think there are any correlations between their intake and their memory or attention span. It seems like a good way of tying the course content into their own lives and habits as learners.

Rob also has some material about how people with different kinds of mental illness—depression or 'generalised anxiety disorder', for example—may learn differently, and how leisure centres might support their learning more effectively. His own brother suffers from severe depressions, and Rob feels strongly that students should learn to understand more about mental health issues. Again, he is going to try to link this with their own learning, maybe through a visualisation exercise, getting them to look at how their mental functioning is affected by their moods (how anxiety prevents you from concentrating, for example, or how depression makes you focus your attention inwards rather than outwards). He starts thinking about how this applies to himself, and wonders if he could set up a public action research project on his own moods for the students to observe . . .

Back in Beckley Road, satisfied that she has her plans well in place, Rita Salbiah drifts off into memories of her own summer break in that 'alternative holiday community'—falling off her wind-surfing board with whoops of laughter; letting herself be massaged by the guy with cerebral palsy; heart-to-hearts in a dark corner of the bar with a new friend; and—Horrors!—prancing around as a scantily-clad Aretha Franklin singing 'Respect' in the cabaret. Things she would never have dreamed of doing a few years ago. And things she would never dream of telling her colleagues or her children at Beckley Road. Some things really are private . . .

Section 3b

Building learning power in practice

Teaching for learning power

This section gives a systematic introduction to the principles behind BLP teaching. We explore the framework that BLP teachers need to have at the back of their minds, as they explain the approach to their students, plan their activities, comment on students' performance, and demonstrate the four Rs in their own lives.

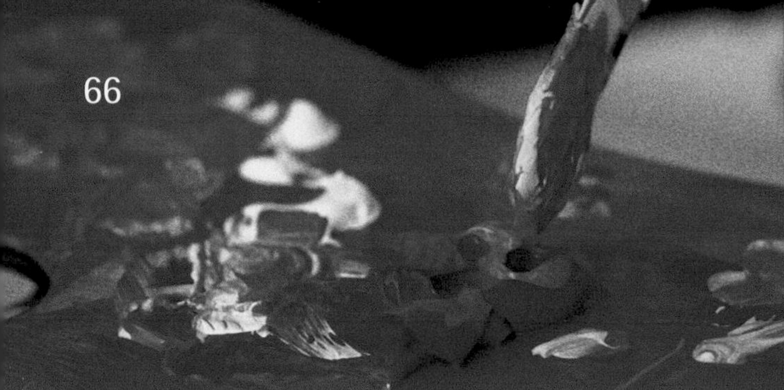

Key points

BLP –

- runs through the whole life of a school
- influences many aspects of classroom life
- is not a quick fix

The learning power teacher's constant question—

'How can I help develop the resilience, resourcefulness, reflectiveness and reciprocity of my students through explaining, commentating, orchestrating and modelling—in the context of this particular topic, with these particular resources and constraints?'

Learning as you teach

As any teacher knows, it's impossible to get it right first time, every time. BLP is no exception. Some good ideas may have to be modified several times before they work with a particular group. One special needs teacher in South Wales tried to get a group of boys to set their own learning-to-learn targets. The way she presented it first was too complicated for them, and it didn't catch on, so she went back to the drawing board and made it simpler. Still it didn't work. She thought about giving up, but then decided to have one more go, making the suggested targets what she felt were far too easy, even for this group with learning difficulties. The next day a colleague walked past the room where the boys were working, and said to the teacher during break 'What on earth have you done with that group? I've never seen them so engaged and enthusiastic.' Not only was it worth persisting, but the teacher had a chance to develop her own resilience, resourcefulness, reflectiveness and reciprocity–and to demonstrate a bit of learning to the boys (and to her colleague).

Teaching for learning power

Putting BLP into action is not a seven-day wonder, a quick fix, or a miracle cure for all ills and difficulties. It is potentially a long journey that starts with a few small steps and is capable of fundamentally shifting the way teachers think, the way they teach, and the whole life and ethos of a school. There are even whole LEAs that are implementing BLP.

The examples over the next few pages illustrate some ways in which schools have been putting BLP into practice. Most of them started life as experiments dreamed up by teachers like Rita Salbiah and Rob George, either on their own or, more usually, in collaboration with like-minded colleagues, keen to develop the spirit of learning-to-learn in their schools and classrooms. Sometimes they have adapted ideas from other approaches. As we have seen, some of the BLP methods overlap with other initiatives that have been developing in educational systems around the world for a few years now. But many are new.

Learning power in the classroom

BLP potentially runs through the whole life of the school and its community. But its base, its engine room if you like, is the classroom. This is where students experience the approach most clearly in relation to their learning of the formal curriculum. That's what we are going to focus on in this section.

BLP influences many aspects of classroom life, including:

- the way teachers explicitly talk to students about the process of learning
- the kinds of activities and discussions which they initiate
- the visual images, prompts and records on the classroom walls
- students' sense of the purpose that lies behind these activities and discussions
- the kinds of questions they are encouraged to ask, and the kinds of follow-up they are expected to make to such questions
- the way teachers respond to students when they are experiencing difficulty or confusion
- the kinds of formal and informal comments and evaluations they make of students' work
- the kind of use that teachers make of classroom assistants and other adults who may find themselves in the classroom
- the kind of homework that is set, and how the process of doing homework is discussed with the students
- above all else, perhaps, the way teachers present themselves as learners—what kind of model or example they offer, for instance when things are not going according to plan, or when a question arises that they had not anticipated.

Teachers do many things in order to create their own distinctive 'classroom culture'. Some of these are the outcome of straightforward conscious choices: whether to place students in working groups, or to let them choose their own partners, for example. Others may reflect less conscious habits of communication or emotional reaction—how they respond to wrong answers or cheeky interruptions. Out of all these aspects of teachers' style, there are some that impinge on

The learning-power palette

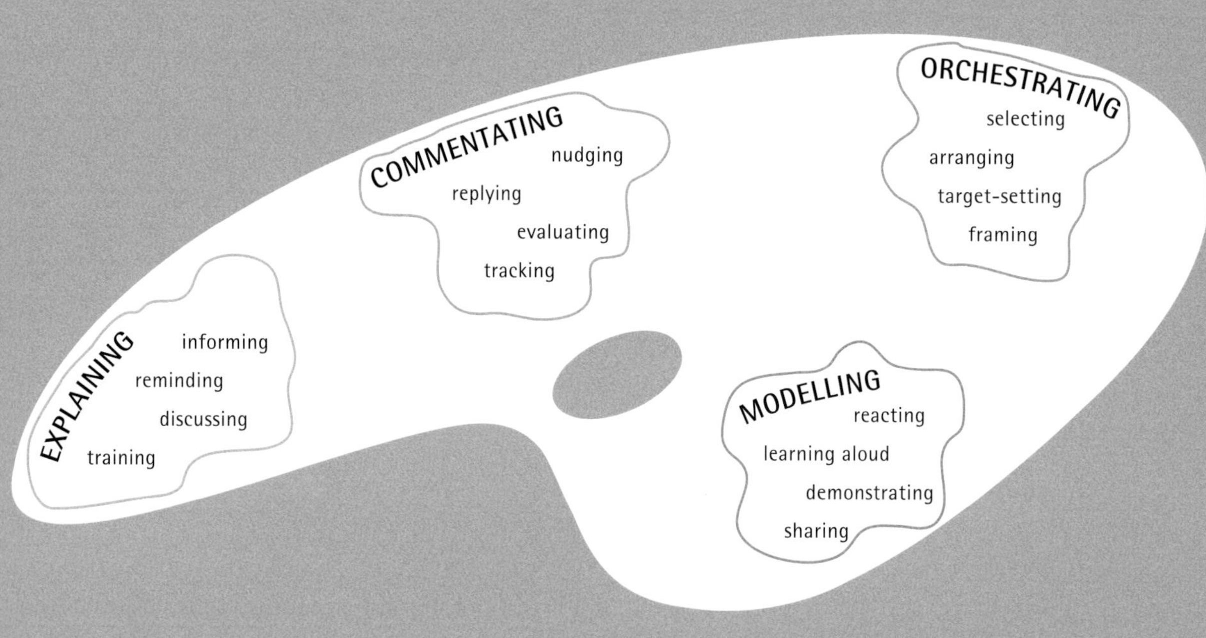

Teaching for learning power

the development of learning power more than others. Teachers can promote learning power through (a) what they explicitly value and discuss with the whole class; (b) how they talk to groups and individuals about their learning and achievement; (c) the activities they select; and (d) what they themselves model about learning. We call these four general categories explaining, commentating, orchestrating and modelling. Each of these has a number of key components which are summarised below, and spelled out in greater detail over the next few pages.

Explaining	– **telling students directly and explicitly about learning power**
Informing	– making clear the overall purpose of the classroom
Reminding	– offering ongoing reminders and prompts about learning power
Discussing	– inviting students' own ideas and opinions about learning
Training	– giving direct information and practice in learning: tips and techniques
Commentating	– **conveying messages about learning power through informal talk, and formal and informal evaluation**
Nudging	– drawing individual students' attention towards their own learning
Replying	– responding to students' comments and questions in ways that encourage learning to learn
Evaluating	– commenting on difficulties and achievements in learning-positive ways
Tracking	– recording the development of students' learning power
Orchestrating	– **selecting activities and arranging the environment**
Selecting	– choosing activities that develop the four Rs
Framing	– clarifying the learning intentions behind specific activities
Target-setting	– helping students set and monitor their own learning power targets
Arranging	– making use of displays and physical arrangements to encourage independence
Modelling	– **showing what it means to be an effective learner**
Reacting	– responding to unforeseen events, questions, etc. in ways that model good learning
Learning aloud	– externalising the thinking, feeling and decision-making of a learner-in-action
Demonstrating	– having learning projects that are visible in the classroom
Sharing	– talking about their own learning careers and histories

Key points

- Make learning explicit
- Take students behind the scenes of learning
- Continually reinforce the message
- Keep the message fresh

The learning-power palette

Explaining

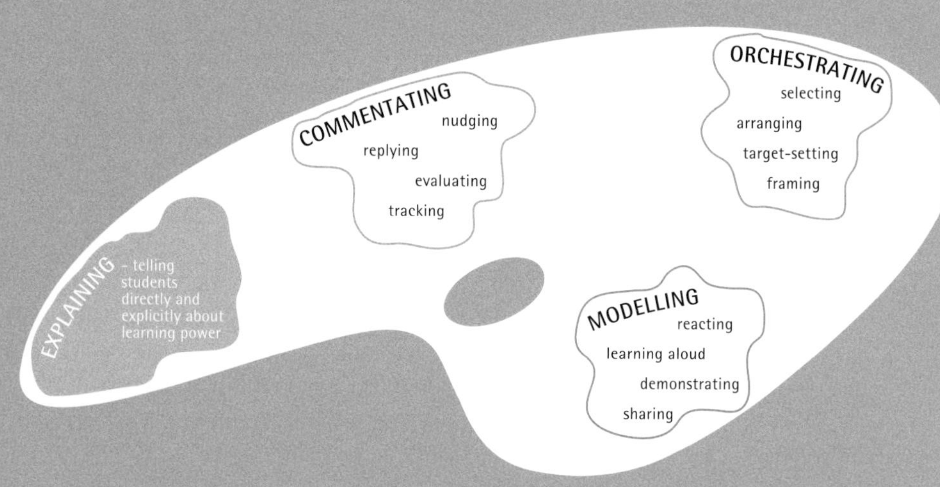

informing	making clear the overall purpose of the classroom
reminding	offering ongoing reminders and prompts about learning power
discussing	inviting students' own ideas and opinions about learning
training	giving direct information and practice in learning: tips and techniques

Explaining: telling students directly and explicitly about learning power

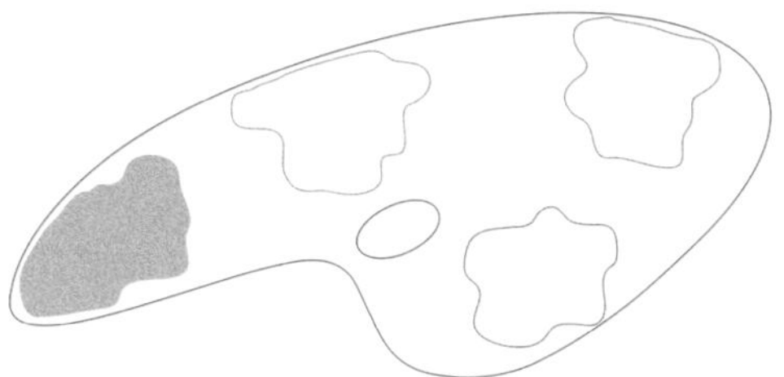

The first aspect of teaching that focuses on building learning power is explaining. Of course, explaining and telling students things is the teacher's stock-in-trade. Whether it's adding fractions, the French past tense, or health and safety in swimming pools, teachers are well practised in conveying information and ideas. BLP teachers, however, learn to discuss the learning process itself, and make learning an explicit theme that runs across whatever subject-matter they may be dealing with. Aspects of learning can be discussed directly, and if teachers want their students to engage more in certain kinds of discussion and debate, for example, they can explain exactly what they want and why it matters. There is plenty of scope to make the nature of learning part of the explicit subject-matter of any lesson. We group these aspects of explaining into four which we call: **informing, reminding, demonstrating** and **training.**

Informing

The first thing BLP teachers have to do is openly set the scene for the students. The students have to know what learning power is, and to understand that in this classroom (whatever they are being told elsewhere) building learning power is a real, ongoing priority. It is part of the BLP approach that students are taken 'behind the scenes', so that they know what their teachers' intentions and values are. There is little or nothing in BLP that cannot be talked about overtly in the classroom.

Section 1b of this book offers a framework for talking about learning power that can readily be shared with students. The language teachers use, and the amount of detail into which they go, will vary depending on the age and sophistication of their classes. Five-year-olds know what it means to persevere. 18-year-olds can understand the uses of imagination. Everyone can engage with the question of when it is better to struggle on your own, and when to seek help.

Reminding

Talking about BLP is not something that happens at the beginning of the year, and then quietly disappears into the background. It has to be followed through, so that it becomes embedded in students' routine habits, attitudes and expectations. If teachers do not keep reminding students what the BLP priorities are, and reinforcing the BLP messages, attention will inevitably drift back to the more familiar agenda of concentrating only on the content, the subject-matter, and ignoring the process. (They revert to discussing the construction of the dumb-bells, and away from seeing how they can be used to build up strength.) If BLP only surfaces as the subject of the occasional pep-talk, and gets forgotten in between, students won't take it seriously. Like all of us, they are quick to spot good intentions that don't translate into practice.

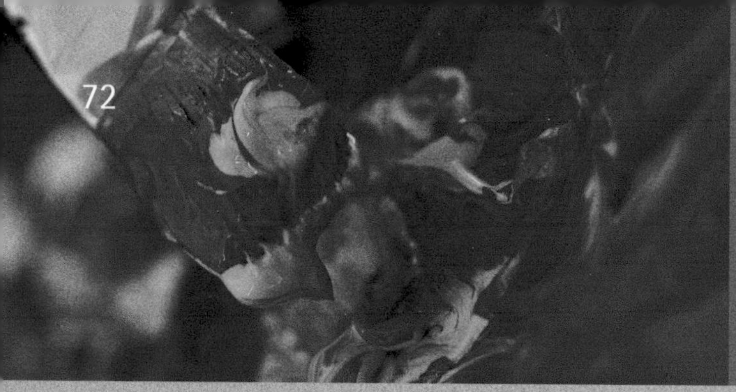

Key points

- Feed in information about the brain and learning
- Adopt the 'mayonnaise' model
- Encourage discussion about learning

Prompts to unstick learning

In Beverley Ball's year six classroom you will see a big poster called 'What good learners do'. This is a list of ideas that the students themselves have generated, about what they can do to help their own learning—especially when they get stuck. Whenever a student gets into difficulty, they have got used to looking at the poster to see if there is anything there that might help them. The first thing Beverley will ask is 'Have you looked at the poster?' and if they have forgotten, they are prompted to do so before turning back to the teacher for help.

The poster is a work in progress. The students have got into the habit of seeing if they can think of new things to add to it. (This means they are developing the reflectiveness to spot when they are using a useful strategy or displaying a positive attitude. It also gives a visual record of the class's resourcefulness in coming up with good ideas.)

The other thing that this poster does is tacitly reinforce the idea that 'getting stuck' is a normal and regular occurrence—even for 'good learners'. However good a learner you are, there is always something more you can learn to strengthen your own learning. Through the use of devices such as this, the message in Beverley's classroom is that finding learning hard does not mean you are lacking in 'ability'. It means that there is an opportunity to develop one or more of the four Rs. Students in that classroom are less ashamed of their difficulties and mistakes than they used to be, and therefore more willing to ask questions, stay engaged, and 'have a go'.

What good learners do

Listen to others

Ask as well as answer questions

Co-operate with others

Ask yourself where you went wrong and why

Don't give up when you are stuck. You could

- read the question again
- split the question into smaller bits
- ask someone who has a similar problem
- ask yourself: what do I know already that could help me?
- go on to another question and come back to the bit you are stuck on at the end

Explaining . . .

The best way of reminding is to keep the message fresh. Repeating the same formulae quickly becomes tedious for both teacher and students. One way of refreshing the BLP perspective is to keep feeding in titbits of new information. The media are full of reports and articles about the brain and the mind, which can be used as the basis for a quick review of the learning-to-learn idea. One week there might be an article in the paper about the use of visualisation in sports coaching; another, a TV programme about the way learning can dry up in Alzheimer's Disease, or about how babies learn to walk or talk. It should be possible to find a few minutes each week to draw students' attention to such information.

Some teachers choose to focus on different aspects of learning power one at a time, and to feed in information, and offer activities, that just relate to that particular ability. Especially at the beginning, when students are getting used to the idea, this can be helpful. After the initial overview, taking each aspect in turn and taking time to ensure that students have grasped what it is about, gives them a firmer foundation to build on, and stops them getting overwhelmed or confused.

BLP makes use of the 'mayonnaise' model of teaching and coaching. When you start to make mayonnaise, you have to add the oil a drop at a time, and make sure it is well beaten in before adding the next drop. Add the oil too fast and it curdles—it refuses to blend in. So, when trying to coach any skill, you start by adding information slowly, and giving lots of time for practice and discussion. If you talk too much, the knowledge separates out from students' spontaneous way of learning, and doesn't make a practical difference. After they have got the hang of it more securely, then you can add information in larger amounts.

If knowledge just stays as knowledge, the BLP approach has failed. That's why the other three aspects of teaching—commentating, orchestrating and modelling—are at least as important as explaining. They all aid the blending process. If ideas don't take root, and if they don't last and deepen, and begin to spread throughout all areas of students' lives as learners, then the main intention has not been fulfilled.

Discussing

But BLP teachers don't just feed information about learning to their students. They actively encourage them to chew it over, digest it, and question it. It is essential to the BLP approach that knowledge about learning to learn is created by teachers and their students, not just consumed by them. In this way, the ideas keep being explored, questioned and developed, and this creates a sense of ownership, generates a feeling of progress and momentum, and it is also another way of keeping the approach fresh.

It is important that all ideas about learning power are not presented as if they were a universal truth, or the latest certainties discovered by fiercely clever people in laboratories. They are to be tried out and evaluated, and if necessary modified or abandoned. Such ideas work if they fit into the overall culture of the classroom; they cannot of themselves create that culture. For example, it is easy to dish out a questionnaire on learning styles or multiple intelligences, and to get students to identify their own preferred style or their profile of intelligences.

Key points

- Encourage a 'could be' frame of mind
- Recognise students' ways of doing things
- Coach the how and why of learning skills

Celebrating learning power

Another thing you will see in Beverley Ball's room is what her students call 'The Learning Wall'. It is some large sheets of coloured paper on the wall on which are stuck a whole lot of Post-its. Each Post-it records a moment when one of the students was observed—or better still, caught themselves—operating at the leading edge of their own learning power.

Gerry thought of a new way of doing a multiplication sum.

For the first time, Anya remembered to look at the 'What good learners do' poster before giving up.

Craig stayed engaged with his writing for five whole minutes.

Each of these achievements may not look very spectacular from the outside, but for Gerry, Anya and Craig they are moments to be proud of—and the Post-it records and celebrates those moments. Because it is public, the Learning Wall also represents progress for the class as a whole, and this helps to foster the team spirit. Finally, children regularly browse the Learning Wall and gain inspiration and ideas about how they can improve their own learning from the recorded achievements of their friends. As the children get used to the idea of catching themselves (and each other) at the leading edge of learning, so their self-awareness grows too.

In a kindergarten in New Zealand, these leading edge vignettes—what Professor Margaret Carr calls 'learning stories'—were often captured in a photograph. Four-year-old Kylie, having climbed to the top of the climbing frame by herself for the first time, caught sight of Margaret across the playground and yelled 'Quick! Get the camera!'

Explaining . . .

Many people enjoy these kinds of 'Know thyself' quizzes. But they may do more harm than good if they leave students feeling that they have been labelled and boxed, and that what they lack they will always lack.

In the BLP approach, such ideas are always discussed and critiqued. Just because Howard Gardner is a Professor at Harvard, it doesn't necessarily mean that there are only seven forms of intelligence in this part of the world. Maybe Year 11 at St Edmund's can come up with another one. And maybe they can e-mail Professor Gardner and see what he thinks. In BLP, frameworks are used mindfully, not mechanically—and that includes the four Rs, and everything else in this book.

Students are continually encouraged to meet all ideas with a 'could be' frame of mind, rather than an expectation of unimpeachable truth. BLP teachers get used to using the language of possibility rather than certainty. Remember Ellen Langer's demonstration of how the use of 'could be' language expanded students' creativity (page 26). If you are told something as if it were incontrovertible fact, your job is to understand it, learn it, master it—but not to question it or play with it. On the other hand, if you are told that 'This is one way of looking at the situation' (and Muslims or biochemists or creationists have a different view), you are much more likely to ask genuine questions. (From the BLP perspective, there is no more need for Darwinists to be frightened of students seeing how evolution looks from a creationist point of view than vice versa.)

Training

As well as explaining and discussing ideas, BLP teachers are also on the lookout for useful hints, tips and techniques which they can pass on to their students—or, even better, which students can pass on to each other. Studies show that students often know a variety of ways for doing sums, or for memorising lists, but sometimes this lay knowledge is not recognised, and not allowed to surface in the classroom. Teachers may believe that they have the *right* or the *best* way of doing long division, and all other ways are bad habits. They may be, but why not bring them into the open, and subject them to testing and debate? There are a host of ways of boosting memory, for example. Master them, and like the World Memory Champion you too could easily remember the order of a pack of cards, or the long line of prizes whipping by on the game-show conveyor belt. Or even those French verbs or the kings and queens of England.

Training does not always involve teaching students new tricks, though. Sometimes it simply means being explicit about what you want them to do, as learners, and why. Teachers sometimes complain that their students are not very good at listening to each other (let alone to the teacher). This can usually be remedied with some explicit instruction and explanation, and concerted practice over a few weeks. The whole class can talk about what 'good listening' involves; how it feels when you are listening well, or being listened to; and what the cues are that tell you when someone is really listening (or not). It's not that they can't do it. It's just that they may never have been explicitly coached in the how and the why of it.

Key points

- Comment on the processes and outcomes of learning
- Encourage and support
- Prompt thinking about how to tackle a task
- Stimulate exploration of different approaches

The learning-power palette

Commentating

nudging	drawing individual students' attention towards their own learning
replying	responding to students' comments and questions in ways that encourage learning-to-learn
evaluating	commenting on difficulties and achievements in learning-positive ways
tracking	recording the development of students' learning power

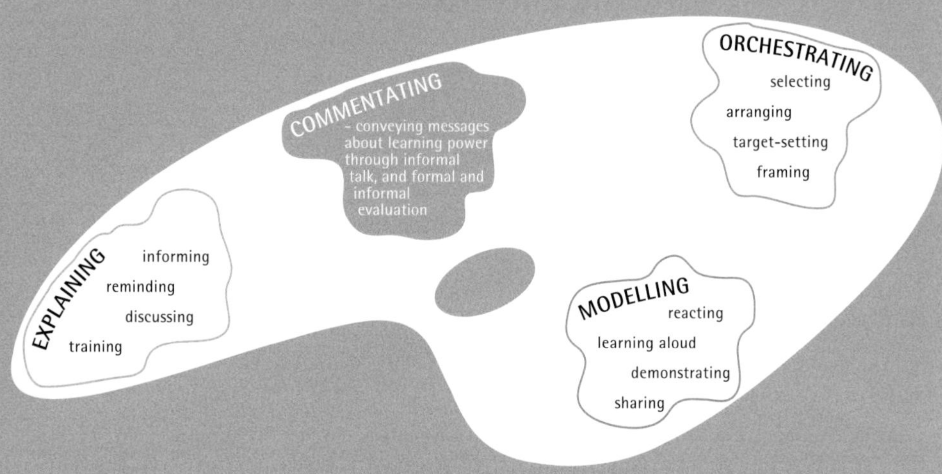

Commentating: conveying messages about learning power through informal talk, and formal and informal evaluation

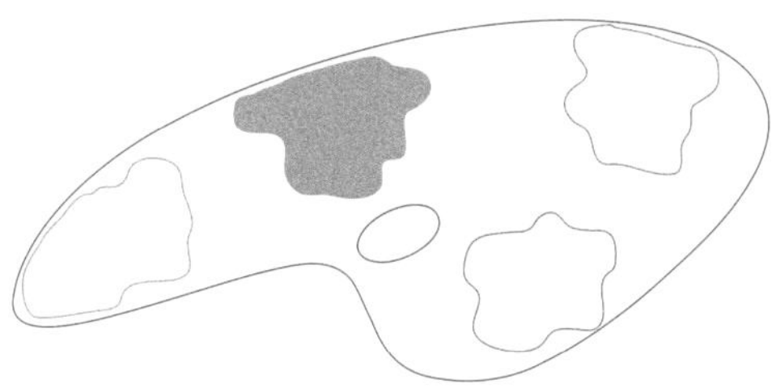

Commentating is also a kind of teacher talk, but a different kind. It refers to the formal and informal reactions teachers have to each student's learning and achievement, and the evaluations they offer back to them. Formally, this includes their written marking, and the reports they write. Informally, it refers to the kinds of interactions they have with students as they are working and learning in the classroom, especially the kind of language they use to comment on students' successes, failures and difficulties. How do teachers respond to wrong answers, or apparently irrelevant questions, for example? Such reactions and conversations convey powerful messages about learning (and about individual students as learners) through language. Precisely because they are implicit, however, such messages may have even more impact than the explicit ones. Commentating can be divided into four aspects: **nudging, replying, evaluating** and **tracking.**

Nudging

Having set the students going on a challenging and interesting activity, BLP teachers interact with them as they go along, commenting not just on outcomes but on their learning methods and processes. Probably their most common forms of interjection are to encourage and support students in their learning, to prompt them to think about how they are tackling the task, and to stimulate them to explore different ways of doing so. These are some of the responses that BLP teachers frequently use.

- 'That's good. Can you see if there's another way of getting the answer?'
- 'How did you do that?'
- 'What do you think would happen if that was x squared rather than just x?'
- 'How could you find out more about that?'
- 'What would be the hardest bit to teach someone else, do you think?'
- 'Try imagining you are that bit of hamburger being digested. How would it feel?'
- 'Does this connect with anything we did last week?'
- 'What do you think is going to happen next?'
- 'Have you looked at the prompt poster?'
- 'Can you think of a way in which you could use this method in your own life?'

The point of each of these kinds of prompt is not to get the students to produce better work—though that will almost certainly happen—but to model the kinds of thought processes that, bit by bit, can be taken in and become part of their own spontaneous way of thinking about learning.

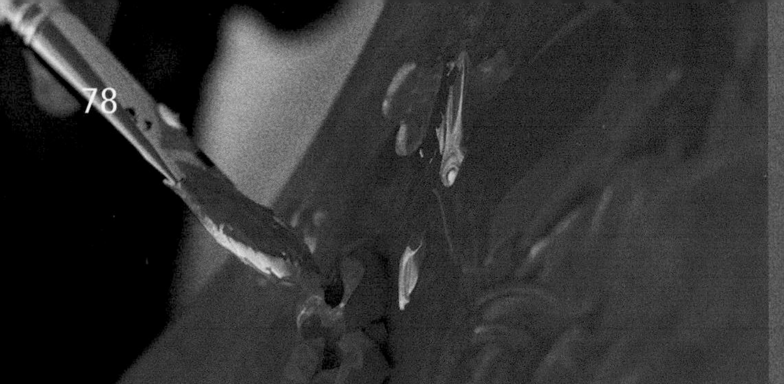

Key points

- Think and talk—learning is learnable
- Allow learners to engage with difficulties
- Welcome questions genuinely

Encouraging Questions

Some ideas to try

Here are some ideas that have successfully increased the amount of student participation in thinking and questioning in the classroom.

- Have a regular 'question time' slot in the school day or week. Students and teacher share any questions that have occurred to them. Special acknowledgement is given to any questions to which nobody, especially the teacher, knows the answer. Out of this can naturally emerge a discussion about different kinds of questions; whether some questions have answers and some do not; what makes a 'good question'; and so on. When there is an odd five minutes, select one of the questions to puzzle away at. See which questions can be worked up into do-able projects, whether for the questioner specifically or for the whole class.
- Have a 'Question Wall' where students and teachers can publicly record their questions. Review them periodically as above.
- Appoint a rotating classroom monitor to record who asks the most questions during a lesson. Or get them to keep track of how much of the time is taken up with 'teacher talk', and how much of that is to do with administration rather than real learning.
- Assign part of the marks for a unit of work on the basis of the questions that students have asked. Get the students to evaluate their own or each others' questions.
- Get the students to set their own tests. For example: divide a section of work into five or six units, and the class into the same number of small groups. Each group has fifteen minutes to come up with three 'fair questions' on their assigned unit, with prepared answers. The questions are compiled into the whole test. After the test, as well as (perhaps) marking their own work, students join in a (sometimes vigorous) discussion about the quality of the questions. Members of the different groups are invited to the front to work through their prepared answers.

RESEARCH TELLS US . . .

'Careless talk costs learning lives'

Jacquelynne Eccles and her colleagues at the University of Michigan have found that the way parents and teachers talk to their children and students can have a major effect on the development of their learning power. In one study, Eccles looked at the way parents interpreted their children's relative success or failure in different subjects. If their son had done well in maths, the parents tended to attribute the success to 'ability', while if the boy had done badly, they were more likely to blame lack of effort. For their daughters, however, it was the other way round. Girls who had done well in maths were praised for having tried hard, while their failures were 'excused' on the basis of lack of ability. ('Never mind, sweetie—you were never going to be a rocket scientist, were you?') Interestingly, the patterns were reversed if the subject in question was English.

It turned out that these comments had a direct, practical impact on the students' subject choices; how they felt about their chances of success; the learning challenges they were willing to undertake; and how much effort they were prepared to put in. Obviously, if you are told several times, by someone you trust, that you just don't have what it takes, you would be stupid to persist, wouldn't you?

Commentating . . .

The language that the teacher uses in these informal, often quite short, interactions, can convey very different messages, some of which will encourage learning-positive ways of thinking, and others, maybe quite inadvertently, will have the reverse effect. The most important instance of this is 'ability' language. BLP teachers try hard to stop themselves thinking and talking as if ability were the problem; and start thinking and talking all the time from the point of view that learning is learnable, and that grappling with learning challenges is more important than any amount of easy success. Every student should be regularly finding learning tough, even the so-called brightest. Otherwise they are wasting their time just as much as if they went to the gym and sat in a corner plaiting their hair.

The language of emotion can also influence the development of learning power, especially resilience, and especially in younger children. If a four-year-old is struggling with a project, hits a snag, and is on the verge of tears, what messages can your verbal (and non-verbal) language convey? If you offer no support at all, the child might abandon the task. But if you run over and rescue her from the situation too quickly and too comfortingly, the message might be that she was right to get upset because failure or frustration are indeed terrible things. Encouragement to persist, suggestion of a period of 'time out' (after which she might like to try again), or a friendly but more matter-of-fact kind of response could all give a more learning-positive message. Good learners do not grow by being protected from difficulty, but by engaging with it, and thereby developing their stamina and their skill. (Remember Doreen Arcus's research, page 22.)

Replying

How teachers respond to the questions, suggestions and ideas that students volunteer influences the development of learning power significantly. If teachers want to encourage students to ask questions, and to gain the confidence to share their speculative ideas in public, they have to demonstrate that questions and contributions are genuinely welcome, even if they don't fit neatly with what the textbook says or the timetable allows. One sure way to discourage questions and comments is to say to the contributor: 'That's a really interesting question/comment . . .' and then immediately keep on inviting other contributions until (with an insufficiently disguised sigh of relief) you finally get the response you want, affirm it to the class, and move hastily on to the next item on the pre-set agenda. Teachers who feel that they simply cannot make time to respond more fully to students' questions must accept that they will inevitably be reducing students' interest in being inquisitive, and in participating in and 'owning' what is happening.

Teachers should not underestimate how risky it feels for many students to share their difficulties, questions and half-formed opinions in a classroom discussion. Research by Ian Mitchell of the PEEL project in Melbourne, Australia shows that participation often feels very risky. Interestingly, his research reveals that the major fear is not of being wrong but of 'looking silly'—saying something that is taken as laughable

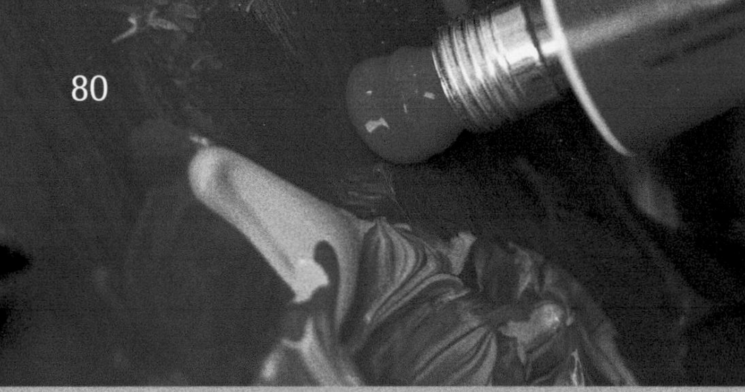

Key points

- Establish four trusts
- Interpret students' difficulties as opportunities to develop learning power
- Develop students' ability and inclination to become their own marker

Students talk about the risks of opening up in class

Interviewer: Why don't you like to talk in front of the whole class, Katie?

Katie: Because I'm scared . . . everybody probably knows what they are doing except me and I don't want to put up my hand and say I don't understand this but . . . if the rest of the class knows it or . . . if it's not the right time or . . . they probably won't but they might laugh.

Interviewer: Do you participate more with other teachers now, Danielle?

Danielle: We've tried it with other classes but they just won't listen—they just say get on with the work . . . they're not interested . . . When the teacher can't be bothered, why should the student?

Interviewer: What does [Mr X] do to put you off asking questions?

Students: He puts pages of notes on the board and tells you to copy them down. If you ask any questions he tells you off . . . he says 'You've just learnt that so how come you have any questions?

The PEEL Project, Victoria, Australia

How marking affects learning

'A raw score on a page demotivates all but the highest achievers.

A raw score and comments, and the vast majority do not even read your comments.

Educative feedback with specific points for improvement is best.'

Professors Paul Black and Dylan Wiliam,
Kings College, London

Commentating . . .

or inappropriate by either teacher or peers. The teacher's job, says Mitchell, is to establish four 'trusts':

- the trust that they will take students' questions and ideas seriously
- the trust that they will communicate to students genuine intellectual respect
- the trust that the confusion that genuine class debates and discussions generate will be eventually and successfully resolved
- and the trust that students will be supportive of each other—'to disagree, but not to ridicule', as Mitchell puts it.

Mitchell is very clear that: 'This [fourth trust] requires clear guidelines, leadership and training from the teacher. If left to themselves, students are not often very good at criticising an idea without criticising the person who proposed it.'

Some examples of ways of encouraging questions are on page 78.

Evaluating

'Ability language' is just one of the hazards that needs to be avoided in offering feedback to students about the quality of their work and the source of their difficulties. Even hint to a student that they are struggling because they lack ability, and you might as well be laughing at them for trying. Once they get the idea that having to try means they are 'not very bright', trying becomes an aversive experience which they will then do their best to avoid—either by choosing tasks that they know how to do easily, or by goofing off or mucking about. BLP teachers interpret students' difficulties as opportunities to develop learning power, not as evidence that they are unintelligent or lazy.

More formally, the way teachers mark students' work also affects their learning development (as well as their learning achievement). In the BLP approach, the objective is to help students develop the ability and the inclination to become their own self-marker. That doesn't mean they don't need feedback. They need to be shown what good work looks like, and guided towards producing it. But the teacher's job is always to make transparent the relevant criteria and processes. As Australian educator Royce Sadler emphasises, this means making clear what is desired and what they have achieved, and helping them see how to close the gap.

Wherever possible, students should get used to being their own first marker, being guided, if necessary, to focus on the original intention behind the product, and to identify for themselves where any areas for improvement can be found. Discussion between peers, in pairs, small groups, or as a whole-class discussion, helps students develop interest, and gain confidence, in this process. Encouraging students to develop the habit of self-evaluation, and to get better at it, strengthens their own powers of reflection and independence, as well as helping them to master the subject matter.

Out of self-evaluation come self-created targets. These targets should relate to what each student is on the brink of being able to do, rather than some remote ideal that they do not yet know

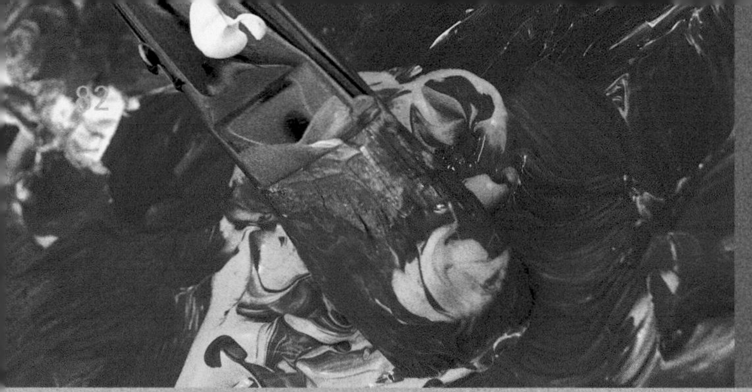

Key points

- Set targets for what the student is on the brink of being able to do
- Track learning power

Freedom to mark as you like

> 'Schools are required to keep records on every child, including information on academic achievements, other skills and abilities and progress made in school . . . There are no requirements about how, or in what form, records should be kept . . . Decisions about how to mark work and record progress are professional matters for the schools as a whole to consider, in the context of the needs of the children.'

DfES / QCA Key Stage 1–2 Assessment Arrangements, 1999

RESEARCH TELLS US . . .

Assessing for learning

Dylan Wiliam and Clare Lee from King's College London worked with 24 secondary science and maths teachers in 6 LEAs to develop new ways of 'assessing for learning'. These included comment-only marking, sharing the criteria of 'good work' with the students, and student peer- and self-assessment. After six months, compared with control groups, these students' performance had risen by between a quarter and a half of a GCSE grade. If such an improvement were to be maintained across a whole school, it would raise the school from the 25th percentile nationally into the top half and possibly the top third. The research shows that busy teachers can find efficient ways to help students learn better, and this has significant pay-off in terms of their achievement.

Commentating . . .

how to achieve. Both teacher and student can keep a note of what these targets are, so that they can be followed up subsequently. It's a good idea to write them on a card that the student can have in full view as they are working on the next assignment, so both they and the teacher know what they are working towards.

Tracking

The kind of cumulative assessment that encourages confidence and commitment is the kind where you can see that you are getting better. It is only in races that athletes compete against each other. In training, they are competing against themselves—developing their own skill and fitness, and striving to improve their personal best. The same applies in the BLP classroom. Students and their teachers are less interested in measuring students' learning power against some external standard, or against each other, and more concerned to track each student's development to see how they are improving.

Unfortunately, to date there are very few tried and tested ways of doing this. Some teachers have successfully developed their own methods, and often they have involved their students in creating their own learning power questionnaire. Developing your own way of tracking the success of the BLP approach is a good way of developing learning power in itself. But it would also be very useful to have instruments available that have been checked for their validity and reliability on a wider scale.

One such instrument, developed recently at the University of Bristol, is called the Effective Lifelong Learning Inventory (ELLI). ELLI enables teachers to take snapshots every so often of the development of their students' resilience, resourcefulness, reflectiveness and reciprocity.

The results can be used in a variety of ways.

- Individual students can keep track of how their learning power is developing (in terms of their self-perception at least).
- Comparing past and present results can form the basis of a reflective discussion between students, or between student and teacher, the outcome of which may be some learning-to-learn targets for the next period.
- The results are also useful in telling BLP teachers whether their intentions are being realised in the classroom.
- And finally, the keeping of such records will help to convince parents, governors and inspectors that the BLP approach is indeed an effective and achievable supplement to more traditional aims for education.

For more information on the ELLI project, see the research panels on pages 102 and 104.

Key points

- Organise the classroom to develop learning power
- Select subject matter to develop the four Rs
- Think 'wild' topics

EXPLAINING
COMMENTATING
ORCHESTRATING
MODELLING

The learning-power palette

Orchestrating

selecting	choosing activities that develop the four Rs
framing	clarifying the learning intentions behind specific activities
target-setting	helping students set and monitor their own learning power targets
arranging	making use of displays and physical arrangements to encourage independence

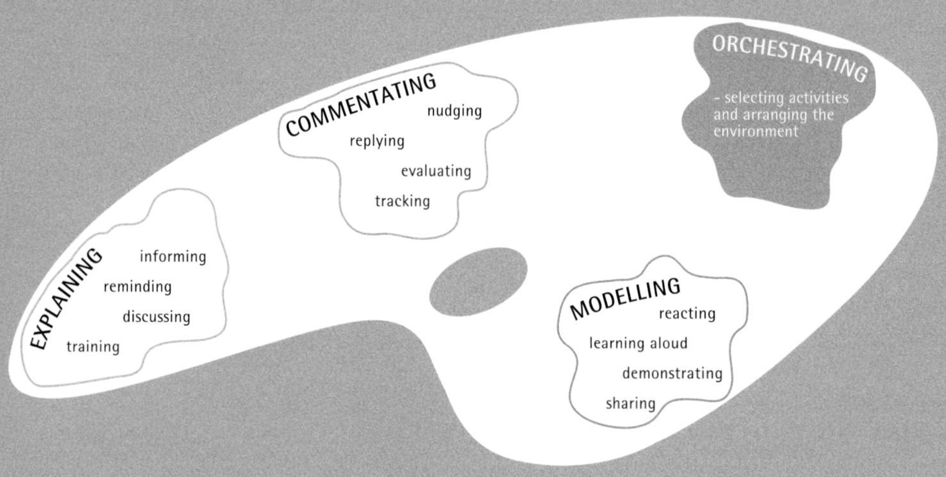

Orchestrating: selecting activities and arranging the environment

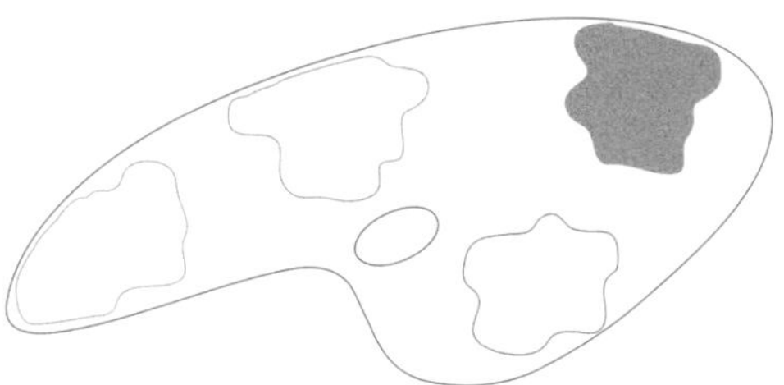

Orchestrating refers to the whole way in which the teacher organises the activities and the environment of the classroom. For the BLP teacher, one of the most important considerations is organising the classroom so that it encourages the development of learning power. There are many other considerations, of course, to do with creating a safe and interesting environment for learning. But none of these must be allowed to squeeze out opportunities for students to strengthen their learning muscles. There are many aspects to orchestrating for learning power, from the kinds of tasks and challenges that are available to what goes up on the walls. BLP teachers may consider:

- what kinds of learning are invited, afforded and encouraged by the activities they offer, and the way their purpose is framed
- how open-ended are the tasks they set
- whether students know what counts as good work
- what kinds of group and solo work the students are to be involved in, and whether they understand the point of varying the social structure of learning
- what kinds of achievements get celebrated, and how
- how they 'decorate' their classrooms
- what the messages are of the way equipment is organised (e.g. are all the six-year-olds tall enough to reach the dictionary?)

We group these aspects of classroom life into four which we call **selecting, framing, target-setting** and **arranging.**

Selecting

Selecting has two aspects: choosing topics to teach, and designing activities through which they are learnt. Some teachers have very little control over the content they are required to teach. Others have rather more. However much elbow room you have, it is important to select subject matter for learning that invites the development of the four Rs. Crudely, topics should be engaging and they should be challenging. It's no use taking people to the gym if the equipment is not inviting enough to 'give it a go', nor if the apparatus is set at levels that are too easy or too hard. Easy is boring; impossible is depressing. Professor David Perkins of Harvard talks about two types of topics: tame ones and wild ones. Much of the curriculum is too tame, he says. To engage and stretch students, they should be presented with subject matter that is a bit wilder—not so pre-digested and neatened up; more intriguing; offering more ways of going about it.

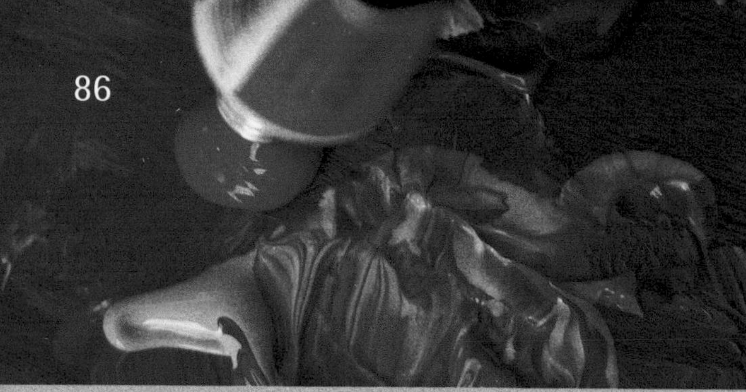

Key points

- Design activities to promote learning power
- Promote discussion on the pros and cons of different methods of learning
- Devote time to students' learning logs
- Encourage learning power targets

'My journey into the unknown'

In Kate Drew's Year 5 class, students spent the last half-hour of every Friday writing quietly in their learning log-book, which they called 'My journey into the unknown'. They wrote about their ups and downs during the week, about the things that they had found that helped them learn, the targets they would like to set themselves over the next week, and the questions about learning that had occurred to them. To get them used to using writing as a reflective tool for their own benefit, Kate told them they could choose whether they wanted her to read what they had written, or not. If they put a star in the corner of the page, that meant it was private. But if the page was not starred, Kate would have a look at what they had written over the weekend, and write back to them—often not with an answer or an evaluative comment, but encouraging them to develop the dialogue with themselves. 'That's a very interesting question, Jenny. I've wondered about why my mood affects how well I can concentrate too. How do you think we could find out more about it? Have a think and write back to me next week.'

This kind of reflective writing is a sophisticated skill in itself, and it takes time to develop. It helps if students are given examples of good practice (appropriate to their learning level), and helped to see, through discussion, what is 'good' about them. It also helps if the teacher models the kind of writing she wants. Continuing examples and modelling are useful for the students who need a little longer to get the hang of it. (It is important, here as elsewhere, not to let the faster students highjack the activity.)

As with all students' work, clear expectations create greater engagement and faster learning. The use of learning diaries and reflective activities needs to be built up gradually in the time and importance that is given to it. To start with, 15 seconds thinking about 'what I need more help with' may be sufficient for a Year 2. For an A-level student, a full written review of her learning strengths and targets for improvement every month might not be too much.

Orchestrating . . .

Most teachers have more freedom over the how of learning than the what. Even if the curriculum is tightly prescribed, the way they present a topic, and the kinds of activities they provide, are more up to them. Lots of slow, clear exposition and dictated notes may, with the right students, reliably achieve good grades in exams. But such teaching only exercises students' powers of sustained attention, accurate transcription and retention, and correct reproduction—only a small part of all that comprises learning power. (If all you do in the gym is work on the development of your pectoral muscles, you are not going to get fit overall.) On the other hand, plenty of discussion and interaction exercise a different muscle group. Varying the size and the composition of the working teams exercises different muscles within this group. Letting students decide the equipment they need for the experiment gets them to think (rather than mindlessly collecting 'one of everything' that has been neatly laid out by the technician).

One of the most powerful forms of activity is to get students to stop and reflect on their learning from time to time. This can take a variety of forms. Students could be asked to spend a couple of minutes in pairs or small groups discussing their learning, what they found difficult, and how they attempted to overcome their difficulties. Then a whole-class discussion might draw out the differences between different groups, and explore the pros and cons of different methods.

'Jacquie and Bill were using diagrams a lot to try to work out the relationships . . . while Kieran and Tien were thinking of real-life experiences that were similar. Which seemed to work best, do you think?'

An increasingly common technique to encourage reflection involves devoting some time to writing in a learning log or reflective journal of some kind. Perhaps once a week, if not more often, time is set aside to review the learning of the previous period, and to consider the lessons learnt and questions raised. 'What did I enjoy most this week?' 'What did I find most difficult, and how did I try to get round the difficulties?' 'What have I noticed about my learning?' And perhaps 'What aspects of my learning power would I like to work on strengthening over the next week?' In this way students can be encouraged to take responsibility for their own learning development, and, in conjunction with the teacher or with their peers, to single out a particular target that they would like to give attention to:

- 'I'd like to see if I can look harder at my mistakes to see what I can learn from them.'
- 'I'm going to experiment with what kind of music helps me concentrate best when I'm doing my homework.'
- 'I want to be able to listen to the other students better.'
- 'I'm going to say when I don't understand, more often.'

Framing

As with all good teaching, BLP teachers make sure that students appreciate the intention behind every activity they are given. When students don't understand the point of an activity—when they don't see how it fits into a bigger picture

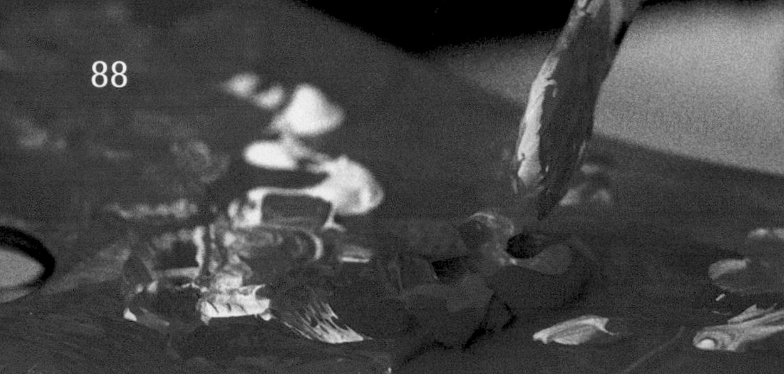

Key points

Design activities with two intentions in mind

- the content of learning
- their contribution to building learning power

Develop learning power bit by bit

Role-playing mountain formation!

Lyn Boyle at Newcomb Secondary College in Melbourne was having trouble getting through to her Year 7s. They didn't quite seem to grasp plate tectonics and mountain-making, no matter how many times she went over it. On the spur of the moment she divided them into groups, gave them a bundle of newspapers, some coloured paper, and told them they could use anything else in the room to help them role-play the formation of at least one type of mountain: 'You have 12 minutes—GO!'

In Lyn's own words, 'Total engagement . . . they argued furiously about what a fault line was . . . how moving land could be represented, and much more . . . Bodies exploded from the centre of mounds of newspaper . . . as they rehearsed volcanic eruption . . . The creation of a rift valley between tables raised to different heights convinced me . . . that they understood far more than they could or would communicate.'

Lyn concluded: 'A major lesson for me. Give students the responsibility, take risks, allow students some freedom to make choices and decisions for themselves . . . They certainly enjoyed the lesson, and several even admitted to me that making the mountains helped them to understand the mountain building process a lot more than their little blue 'comprehension' books had!

(from PEEL seeds 50, p95)

Orchestrating . . .

of learning—it is not surprising that they often just go through the motions. It is obviously more motivating to know why you are doing what you are doing, and to see how it contributes to your own development.

In fact, BLP teachers always have two intentions in mind. The first relates to the content of the learning. They make sure students know why being able to work out the area of an irregular shape, or to translate from one language to another, is a good idea. It may help you in real life, or to gain a qualification, or both. (The activity is 'painting rainbows'; the intention is to learn to blend colours. The activity is 'titrating sulphuric acid against sodium hydroxide'; the intention is to learn laboratory standards of cleaning equipment.)

But BLP teachers also have in mind the learning power intention as well. And they make sure that students know how each activity can contribute to their developing learning power. So as they are learning and working on an activity, students know how struggling with these equations, or this essay, can be helping to develop their learning muscles or learning stamina. The BLP intention behind both painting rainbows and careful titration might be **attentive noticing**; or it could be **asking questions** or **working in teams**. Whichever it is, students should have a sense of what it is they are working on.

Target-setting

Just as athletes can motivate and focus themselves by setting targets, so can developing learners. They might decide, with their teacher's help, to focus for the next half-term on improving their skills and dispositions in any one of the four Rs—asking questions, sustaining concentration, working with others, being more strategic, and so on. It is much easier to improve when both the student and the teacher know what aspect of learning power is being prioritised. Target-setting helps students to work on different aspects in rotation. If you try to work on everything at once, you quickly get overwhelmed, confused and disheartened. Remember the mayonnaise model of teaching and learning. Setting yourself clear targets, one at a time, is a very good way of blending ideas into practice and preventing them curdling.

The other problem with good intentions, as we all know, is that they are inclined to get forgotten in the heat of the moment. BLP teachers can help their students keep their targets in mind in a variety of ways. When they mark work, they can focus their comments specifically on that student's current target. (Other desirable features will get attention in due course.) They can offer verbal prompts as part of their informal commentary. Or they can provide—or get students to create for themselves—visible prompts to keep on their desks as they work: a file card with a few key words on it, or (as in one classroom in Cardiff) a laminated 'place mat' for each of the students, decorated in their own way.

Tracking tools, such as the Effective Lifelong Learning Inventory, can be used to guide and support target setting. For example, one teacher devised her own BLP questionnaire, and gave it to the students in her class at the beginning of

Key points

Use classroom walls to

- record learning power achievements
- celebrate progress in learning power
- display prompts to 'unstick' learning

WILF and TIB

Shirley Clarke at the Institute of Education in London has a device for helping teachers communicate their intentions and purposes clearly to the students, called the WILF and TIB board. It is simply a white board that lives in a front corner of the classroom that has on it in indelible marker a cartoon dog (WILF) and a cat (TIB). Both WILF and TIB have big bubbles coming out of their mouths, and the bubbles have to be filled at the start of each activity.

WILF stands for 'What I'm Looking For . . .' and explains what specific skill is being practised, and what counts as doing it 'well'. The activity is writing about your holiday, but 'What I'm looking for is the correct use of capital letters and full stops', or 'the use of vivid and interesting adjectives'. WILF establishes what we are learning to . . .

TIB stands for 'This Is Because . . . ' and it is where the teacher explains why this skill is useful (in real life), and how it fits into the Big Picture of the developing learner. 'And this is because it will contribute to your ability to communicate clearly, and use writing as a 'theatre' for developing your own thoughts.' TIB tells the students what they are learning for.

While students are still getting used to WILF and TIB they may need to be reminded of what the bubbles say while they are carrying out the activity. Once established, more adventurous teachers can encourage their students to remind them if they forget to do WILF and TIB, or even to refuse to undertake an activity till they know what the purpose and the value are. After they are used to the procedure, students can even be encouraged to guess what WILF and TIB are going to say, and make up their own bubbles—thus getting in the habit of thinking for themselves what the point and value might be.

Orchestrating . . .

the autumn term. The items were statements like 'I like it when I have to try hard', or 'I can think of things to do when I am stuck', and students had to rate them in terms of how often they were applicable to themselves: Almost Never, Occasionally, Sometimes, Often, Almost Always. When they had filled in the questionnaire, students were asked to talk to a neighbour about their responses (they were already used to this kind of conversation), and pick out one statement they would like to score better on by half-term. They tried to think *how much better* they thought they could get in that time, and this became their target. Then, after half-term, they were given a clean version of the questionnaire again to fill in, which they then compared with their earlier version to see if their intentions had borne fruit. If results were disappointing, they discussed why that might be—it was harder than they thought, perhaps, or they didn't think their questionnaire response gave a fair picture—and they could adjust their target or choose a new one. Comparing the two sets of responses overall also gave the teacher valuable information about the extent to which her BLP intentions were being realised.

Arranging

The final thing to consider under this heading is the nature of the classroom environment. Do the images and messages reinforce the concern with learning power? Does the arrangement of furniture invite and encourage the right kinds of learning interaction? Are the resources available to help students become more independent?

For example: it is helpful to use the walls of the room

- to provide a cumulative record of the class's learning achievement
- to celebrate both individual and collective progress
- and to display public prompts that students can use to extend their learning, or to kick-start it when they have got temporarily stuck.

By recording good learning ideas in this public form, students can be encouraged to 'look to the prompt sheet', as a reminder of what they might try, before they call on the teacher to help them out. As this habit becomes second nature, so students' resilience and resourcefulness grow.

During the popularity of the television quiz show *Who Wants to Be a Millionaire?*, some teachers called these sorts of prompts the students' 'lifelines' which, just like 'Phone a friend' or 'Ask the audience', they can use when they are stuck or unsure. At the end of lessons, the class can review who used which lifelines, how many times, and which were the most popular or successful. The class can make up its own rules, like 'You have to have used "Read the poster" and "Ask a friend" before you can use "Ask the teacher".' 'You can have three designated friends (or learning buddies), but you can't use any one of them more than twice in any lesson.' Whatever goes up on the walls, it is important to make use of it in the daily life of the classroom, otherwise it rapidly becomes invisible.

Key points

- Demonstrate the habits and inclinations of a good learner
- Be a confident 'finder outer'
- Say 'I don't know' without getting defensive

The learning-power palette

Modelling

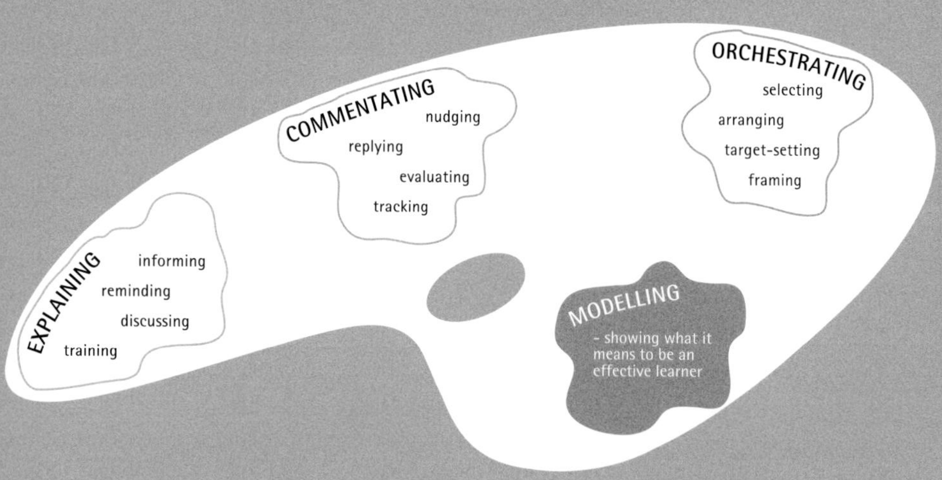

reacting	responding to unforeseen events, questions, etc. in ways that model good learning
learning aloud	externalising the thinking, feeling and decision-making of a learner-in-action
demonstrating	having learning projects that are visible in the classroom
sharing	talking about their own learning careers and histories

Modelling: showing what it means to be an effective learner

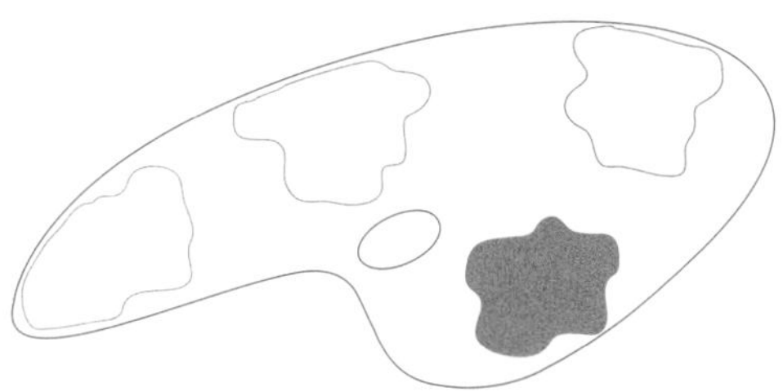

The final aspect of their teaching on which BLP teachers will want to focus is what they themselves are modelling to their students about being a good learner. Modelling refers to all the ways in which teachers demonstrate to their students the presence or absence of learning power in their lives, as well as its nature. They can ask themselves:

- 'How much do I "learn aloud"—externalise my own exploratory thinking—in front of the students?'
- 'How do I react when things do not go according to plan?'
- 'To what extent do I reveal to the students the thinking that went into organising a lesson one way rather than another?'
- 'How do I respond to questions I can't answer—am I thrown by them?'
- 'How much could I reveal about my own learning projects—with all their ups and downs?'

The attitudes, values and interests that a teacher involuntarily displays in the course of a lesson constitute arguably the most powerful medium through which the messages of learning rub off on students.

A BLP teacher's job is as much to demonstrate the habits and inclinations of the good learner as it is to be knowledgeable and in control. Traditionally it has been the teacher's role to demonstrate mastery of the subject, and to be able to answer any questions which the students may throw up. Beginning teachers still tend to worry that they will lose respect from the students (and maybe from senior teachers and parents too) if they do not 'know their stuff' through and through.

But the professionalism of the BLP teacher must allow them to show students what it is to be a confident 'finder-outer' as well as a 'knower'.

And if students or their parents need to have their attitudes and expectations changed somewhat, then that becomes part of the teacher's and the school's responsibility.

Modelling can be divided into four aspects: **reacting, learning aloud, demonstrating** and **sharing.**

Reacting

How teachers respond when the unexpected happens in the classroom tells their students a lot about their teacher's learning power. For example, BLP teachers ought to be able to model a fair degree of resilience. They need to be able to say 'I don't know' without getting defensive, blustering or hiding behind the tried-and-tested formulations of the textbook. Ellen Langer

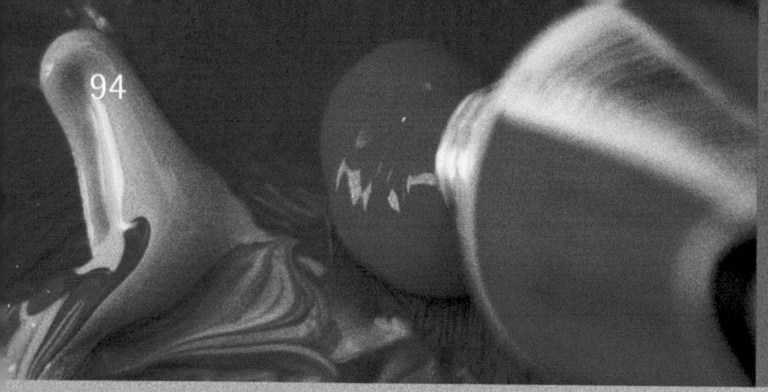

Key points

- Share thinking behind lesson planning
- Seek feedback on your teaching
- Use the techniques you expect students to use
- Model the thought and emotional processes learners go through

A learning power mind map

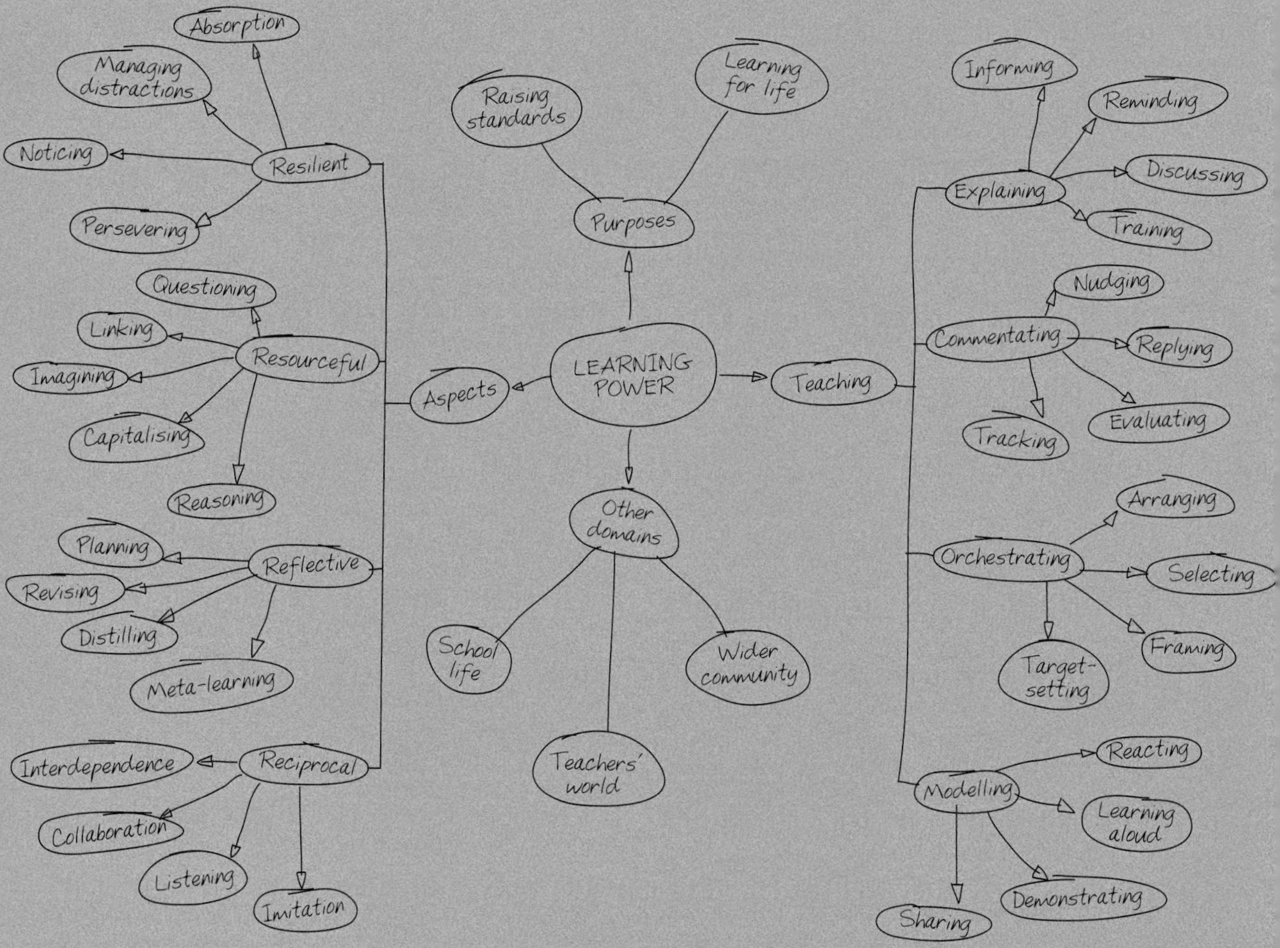

- LEARNING POWER
  - Purposes
    - Raising standards
    - Learning for life
  - Aspects
    - Resilient
      - Absorption
      - Managing distractions
      - Noticing
      - Persevering
    - Resourceful
      - Questioning
      - Linking
      - Imagining
      - Capitalising
      - Reasoning
    - Reflective
      - Planning
      - Revising
      - Distilling
      - Meta-learning
    - Reciprocal
      - Interdependence
      - Collaboration
      - Listening
      - Imitation
  - Teaching
    - Explaining
      - Informing
      - Reminding
      - Discussing
      - Training
    - Commentating
      - Nudging
      - Replying
      - Evaluating
      - Tracking
    - Orchestrating
      - Arranging
      - Selecting
      - Framing
      - Target-setting
    - Modelling
      - Reacting
      - Learning aloud
      - Demonstrating
      - Sharing
  - Other domains
    - School life
    - Teachers' world
    - Wider community

Modelling . . .

at Harvard has shown that, in the world of commerce, project team members value a quality in their team leaders that she calls 'confident uncertainty'. Leaders who possess this quality are able simultaneously to inspire confidence that they know where they are going, and that the problem will be solved (on time and within budget!), and to acknowledge that they are not completely sure how they are going to get there, but they will value support and collaboration in figuring out how to make it happen.

Teachers can develop the same kind of quality, and once their students have adjusted their expectations (if needs be), they too seem to welcome the opportunity to see, and respect, their teachers as learners as well as founts of knowledge. Of course, teachers know much more than the students do (about many things), and should not pretend otherwise. But they are not omniscient, and have no need to appear to be. Many of the teachers I have worked with have said that, even without intending to, they have just found themselves growing much more comfortable with saying 'I don't know'.

The more they are willing to take their students—especially older ones—behind the scenes of the teachers' world, and share with them some of the uncertain thinking behind their lesson planning, the more teachers may well find that the students are not only willing but surprisingly able to share some of the responsibility for planning the route they need to take to get there. After one teacher took the risk of asking her class for feedback on her teaching, they enthusiastically volunteered to *help her become a better teacher!* They contributed plenty of good ideas—and not surprisingly became more engaged in their lessons as well.

It helps if teachers practise what they preach when it comes to learning. If they are going to encourage their students to use mind maps, they should be able to 'put their money where their mouth is', and show them their own mind maps of the current lesson, of the term's work, or of how the major concepts that they want to get across relate to each other. (The mind-map opposite summarises the major concepts of the BLP approach.) There are many more teachers who enthusiastically advocate mind-mapping to their students than use it themselves; and more who use it than demonstrate explicitly to their students how and why they find them useful.

Learning aloud

Reacting is more to do with the involuntary emotional and value messages that teachers give; learning aloud refers to their ability to model to their students the kinds of thought (and emotional) processes that learners go through, usually covertly. This is important, because a lot of the skill of learning only manifests itself in the inner world of the learner. Of course, attitudes and habits are, to an extent, publicly revealed in what you choose to do, how you go about it, and what you say. But equally, learning power is also about how you deal internally with the choices, challenges and frustrations that crop up in the course of learning.

Key points

- Share your learning projects with students
- Show your multiple drafts
- Talk through your frustrations
- Work alongside students
- Verbalise your thought processes

Modelling learning

American mathematics educator Allan Schoenfeld regularly holds 'maths learning masterclasses' with groups of college students, in which they are invited to throw unrehearsed maths problems at him which he then attempts to solve on the spot. As he does so he has learned how to learn aloud, verbalising his thought processes as he explores possible ways he might tackle the problem. 'I could use algebra probably, but it might be easier to try it first with a diagram of forces . . . Let's see what kind of picture we get if we put in simple values for x, y and z . . .' And so on.

As they muse aloud, teachers like Schoenfield also have the opportunity to show that they think in terms of learning-to-learn (rather than ability) language, and 'could be' (rather than unequivocally is) language. Through these kinds of real-time learning demonstrations, BLP teachers are able to model all aspects of learning power, especially resourcefulness and reflectiveness.

> 'The only rational method of educating is to be an example. If you can't help it, be a warning example.'
>
> Albert Einstein

Modelling . . .

Opportunities for learning aloud present themselves in the context of reacting to unexpected events as they occur. But they can also be deliberately created by being willing to undertake activities in the classroom to which teachers have not figured out an answer—nor an entirely reliable learning route to an answer—ahead of time.

To be able to do this requires a degree of confidence which teachers may acquire only gradually, but it is possible to start off in quite small ways, and build up to more challenging situations. There are obvious implications here for pre-service and in-service forms of professional development for teachers. They should have plenty of sessions where they get used to reflecting on their own learning methods (both within their particular subject, and more broadly), and practising the kind of learning aloud that they will be doing with their own students.

Demonstrating

One of the problems with conventional schooling is that it delivers knowledge to the students after all the interesting learning has taken place, and all the uncertainty, disagreement and trial-and-error has been squeezed out of it. They do not usually see the dozens of agonised drafts that D H Lawrence went through before he was satisfied with his poem The Snake. They do not hear much about all the years of puzzlement and painstaking observation that preceded Charles Darwin's insights into the process of natural selection. But their teachers have the opportunity to show them, in their own way, what a slow and uncertain process real learning often is.

- It doesn't have to be D H Lawrence or Carol Ann Duffy: any English teacher can show their students the multiple drafts of a short story or a poem they are trying to write.
- Science teachers can set up their own studies in the corner of the lab, and talk their students through the frustration of not being able to get an experiment to work.
- Design teachers can work alongside their students on their own inventions, failing and improving their product as they go along.
- Like Allan Schoenfeld, maths teachers can model for their students what it is like to *be a mathematician.*

Once upon a time, I used to work in what was then called a 'tutorial centre for maladjusted primary school children', under the direction of a wise and kind teacher called Dennis Gell. On my first day, I was rather nervous—I had never worked with primary age children before, let alone those who for a variety of reasons were emotionally and behaviourally challenging. 'Just find somewhere to sit and read a book or something', Dennis suggested when I arrived. Rather relieved not to have to make the running with these unfamiliar kinds of people, I did as he advised. Soon, one of the boys came up to me, obviously curious, and asked what I was doing. 'Just reading', I said. There was a pause. 'What for?' 'Well,' I said . . . and before I knew it I was trying to explain some of the pleasures and purposes that reading afforded me. The boy wandered off after a while, to be replaced by others who also wanted to know what I was up to. Dennis said to me later that this might be the first time that some of these

Key points

- Share previous learning experiences
- Talk about how you felt when learning
- Talk about how you have changed as a learner
- Share your learning role-models
- Explore learning as a continual 'real life' thing

Learning the bagpipes in public

On his first morning as the new head of Staple Hill Primary School, Peter Mountstephen picked up his bagpipes and strode into assembly. Though they had been bought several weeks before, Pete had resisted the temptation to practise. He was a total bagpipe virgin, and he was going to attempt to play them for the very first time in front of several hundred unknown youngsters, not to mention the staff. Peter explained that he couldn't play the pipes, but he wanted to, and he was going to show them, week by week, his progress, and talk to them about his ups and downs. Then he put the bagpipes to his lips and blew. As expected, he made a truly dreadful noise, and after a shocked silence, the students burst into laughter.

Later in the day, in a Year 6 class, Pete went into a little more detail with the students about what he was going to need in order to achieve his musical goal. He was going to need attention and stickability, drawing on what he knew already about musical instruments, time to think about how and what to practise, and the willingness to learn with and from other people—in other words, he was going to have to be resilient, resourceful, reflective and reciprocal. Over the next few days, he visited every class in the school, talking to all the students, including the youngest and those with special needs, about the four Rs. He was modelling and explaining learning power.

The next step was to talk to the teachers about orchestrating and commentating . . .

Modelling . . .

children had ever seen any adult, in the flesh, (including teachers) just reading a book. They had met lots of people who were telling them what a good thing reading was, and who were earnestly trying to get them to read—but very few who were actually demonstrating that reading (other than magazines or newspapers) was something that grown-ups actually did, voluntarily. This brief experience may or may not work any tangible magic with these children, Dennis said, but he was sure that my time spent simply modelling reading had not been wasted.

Sharing

Finally, teachers have the opportunity to make public their own out-of-school learning projects and learning histories. They may tell encouraging war stories about times they felt blocked or stupid, and how they managed to survive and develop. They can demonstrate the ability to laugh at their own ignorance, and take pride in their stickability. They can talk about the interesting things they have learnt through gazing slowly at a picture, or down into a rock pool. They can talk about how they have changed as a learner as they have grown up, and about the ways in which they would still like to change. They can talk about others they know who have been role models of persistence or ingenuity for them, and the impact they have had on their lives. They can talk about the fun of learning together as a group, and the power of quiet stillness too.

Once teachers start thinking about learning as a continual real-life thing, and not just something that requires books and teachers and grades, they find there is no shortage of things they might talk about. Learning to distinguish New Zealand from Australian accents; to diagnose the cause of their new baby's cry; to find their way around a new city; to dance the tango; to talk to someone who is mentally ill; to design a garden; to curb their temper; to tell a cabernet sauvignon from a merlot . . . nobody need be short of learning adventures to discuss.

Key points

- Become a learning coach
- Teach less and allow learning more
- Stimulate learning without pre-empting it

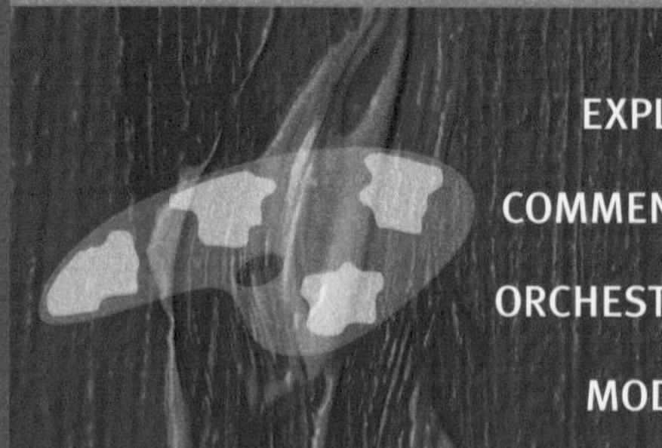

The learning-power palette

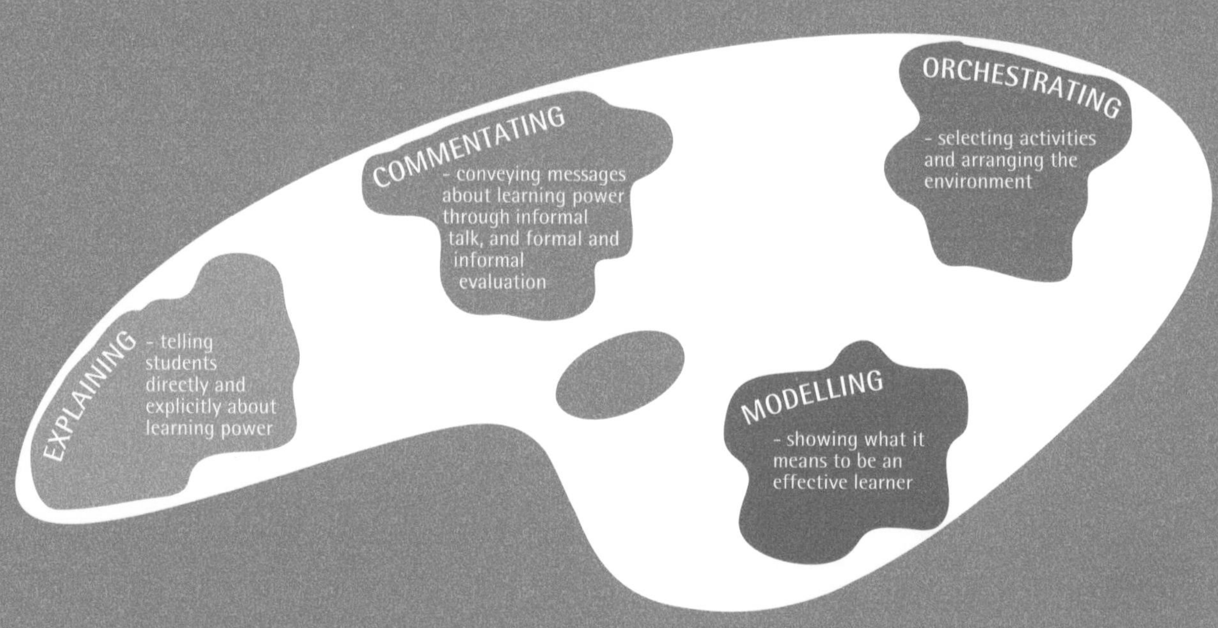

Pulling the threads together

Here we pull together some of the key ideas and principles that are involved in being a BLP teacher.

Being the team coach

Through all the channels we have just discussed, BLP teachers change not just the emphasis of individual lessons or interactions, but the overall climate or atmosphere of their classrooms. If they see their class as a group of young people potentially engaged in improving their learning power, then they become the *team coach.*

- They lay out the BLP *vision* as clearly and attractively as they can, so that as many as possible sign up to the opportunity.
- They *hold* the vision, keeping it in front of the students' eyes, making sure they don't lose sight of the basic aim.
- They aim to create a sense of partnership in which the students *own* the idea of becoming a better learner themselves.
- They cajole and *encourage* students when they lose heart or falter.
- They create a *team atmosphere*, in which students support and encourage each other.
- They monitor and *celebrate* any developments in a student's personal best as a learner—an increase in persistence, say, or a small insight into their own learning.
- They work with individuals to help them set challenging but *realistic targets*, based not on comparison to others but on their own improving performance.

Teaching less and learning more

In general, BLP teachers are always looking for opportunities to teach less, and allow learning more. Results-oriented teachers see nothing wrong in 'chalk and talk'. They are quite right in thinking it can (with the right students) be an efficient way of getting across enough knowledge and understanding for them to perform creditably in the exam. But BLP teachers can't do that, if it means sacrificing the development of all-round learning power. They have to hold back, offering enough to stimulate learning without pre-empting it. Their goal is always to devise activities through which students discover for themselves how the habits of good learning work. Through reflecting on their learning experiences and discussing them with each other, students explore what their different styles or methods are, and pick up other ways of learning and thinking which they might not have thought of by themselves. Through working on learning projects as a team, they discover the value of listening and collaborating. Through being asked to set tests for each other, or to evaluate their own work, they discover how they can improve their own performance without having to rely on continual feedback and correction from the teacher.

Thinking and planning

Learning to be a BLP teacher involves learning to think in two dimensions at once: the **content** dimension and the **learning power** dimension. 'How am I going to get this concept across?' is one question. And at the same time 'What aspects of learning power am I going to focus on?' is the other. Here are some examples of the kind

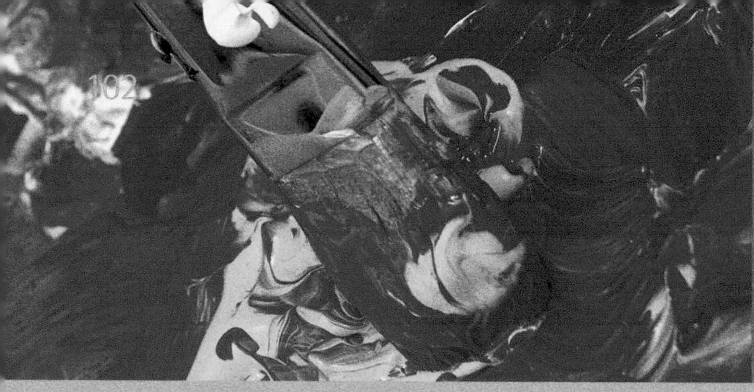

Key points

Think in two dimensions at once

- the content dimension
- the learning power dimension

'I now feel I can support my pupils immeasurably more in taking responsibility not just for the work they do, but for how they do it. I feel I can get them to work at developing, for example, resilience, building up that skill from week to week. I feel that I am no longer a teacher just of English but a teacher of learning as well. This is incredibly positive. Throughout my teaching career I have told my classes that the whole point of education is to make them think for themselves and become better learners. I now have begun to understand how to teach them to do this, rather than just hope that it happens along the way.'

ELLI Advanced Skills Teacher, Secondary School

RESEARCH TELLS US . . .

ELLI—The Effective Learning Power Profile

Research at Bristol University Graduate School of Education has identified seven underlying dimensions of 'Learning Power' from a scientific study that included over 1600 learners from the age of seven through to twenty-five. These dimensions represent the ways in which learners are energised to think, feel and behave in learning situations. The seven dimensions are:

- growth orientation—a commitment to growth and change over time
- meaning making—the capacity to make personally meaningful connections
- critical curiosity—the tendency to want to get below the surface and find things out
- creativity—the capacity to use imagination, playfulness and intuition
- learning relationships—being able to learn with and from other people
- strategic awareness—the capacity to be aware of how learning is happening
- dependence & fragility—the contrast to all the positive dimensions

The ELLI Learning Power Dimensions are 'content neutral' in relation to the formal curriculum and function more as a shadow to the content of what is being learned and thus can be used effectively across subjects and classrooms and beyond. The Effective Learning Power Profile is a range of assessment tools that can be used to track and develop these aspects of Learning Power.

Pulling the threads together . . .

of thinking process that a BLP teacher may go through.

What could I **orchestrate** that would help students work on their **reciprocity / collaboration** in my Year 5 science lessons this week? A different kind of group work maybe? Some images showing scientific research teams working collaboratively for the walls?

How could I **commentate** in a way that would help develop **resourcefulness / imagination** with my Year 11 French group? Maybe I could make an effort to use more 'could be' language when we're discussing this French translation, or exploring the pros and cons of strictly literal versus more poetic interpretations?

What could I **explain** about learning that would focus on **resilience / noticing** in my A-level art class? Maybe I could talk about how Cézanne used to stare at a landscape without moving his eyes until the shapes and colours started to dance into different combinations?

How could I **model reflectiveness / planning** in the context of this unit on simultaneous equations? Maybe I could set up a difficult problem on the board and talk aloud about how I think I could try to tackle it, how long I reckon it might take me, or what resources I suspect I might need. Then maybe I could give them a different problem and orchestrate a similar kind of discussion in pairs.

In practice, of course, the teacher's thoughts are not always as clear-cut as this. Many of the best learning power interventions strengthen more than one of the Rs at the same time. And explaining, commentating, orchestrating and modelling flow back and forth so rapidly, sometimes, in the heat of a lesson, that it becomes pointless to try to keep them apart.

Scaffolding and fading

Students often underachieve not because they don't know what to do, but because they don't do what they know. Just getting someone to appreciate and understand something about learning is only the beginning of their learning-to-learn process. There follows a longer, slower process of dissolving that knowledge into their spontaneous way of reacting. And that needs a continuing process by the coach of prompting and reminding (scaffolding), at first quite frequently and explicitly, then gradually weakening the prompts (fading), so that students develop the habit of doing it for themselves. They are developing the voice of the guiding, prompting coach inside their own heads, so they cease to need external direction. (Of course, this is more likely to work successfully if the voice they are hearing is a friendly, helpful, factual one, not one that is nagging or judging.)

So the job of the BLP teacher can look like this.

1. First you explain something about learning power: you make it clear and explicit.
2. Then you demonstrate it: you show how it works in action.
3. Then you devise some simplified activities in which students can practise the new learning process.

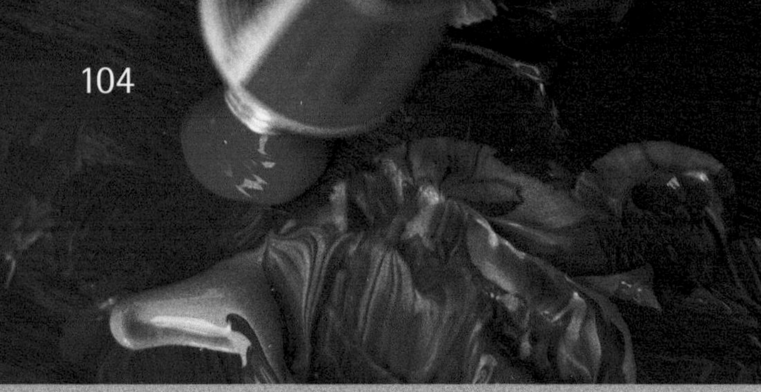

Key points

- Practise elements of learning power in different subjects
- Extend the range of examples beyond school
- Look for links in real life

Working with the ELLI Learning Power Dimensions:

'[has encouraged me to] re-evaluate my teaching approach—a shift from imparting knowledge to acting as a 'coach' guiding, encouraging, suggesting . . . It has helped to focus on my students in terms of their ability to learn and their approach to learning—not simply as students of my own subject'

ELLI Teacher Researcher, Secondary School

'. . . has made me plan lessons which have an ELLI learning intention too . . . I have tried to set aside specific time for children to reflect and for us to talk about all aspects of learning'

ELLI Teacher Researcher, Primary School

RESEARCH TELLS US . . .

Working with the Effective Learning Profile in the classroom

Research at Bristol University Graduate School of Education explored ways in which the ELLI Learning Power Dimensions could be tracked and nurtured as part of everyday life in the classroom. This entailed teachers integrating Learning Power Dimensions into their everyday learning objectives in order to promote learner self-awareness and growth. Sixteen teachers introduced 'learning interventions' to their classes, designed by them to stimulate some of the Learning Power Dimensions. The teachers used the Effective Learning Power Profiles to decide what aspects of Learning Power to focus on for individuals and for the class as a whole. After two terms the children were assessed again to see if their Learning Power Profile had changed.

These classes showed significant increases on the positive ELLI Learning Power Dimensions and they had reduced their profiles on fragility and dependence. In classes where there were no learning interventions, matched to the experimental group, the Learning Profiles actually decreased over the year.

Some of the most important themes from the teachers' work were:

- Teacher professional judgement and commitment
- Positive learning relationships
- Quality of learning dialogues
- Developing a language of learning
- Time for reflection
- Modelling and imitation
- Re-sequencing the content of learning
- A range of self assessment and learning strategies

Pulling the threads together . . .

4. Then (and this is where the bits that often get neglected come in) you make the activities more complex and more ambiguous, so that they have to think which strategy is the right one to apply—they are developing their sophistication both with the method and in telling when it is appropriate.
5. During this stage, you may need to do some reminding and further demonstrating of how the facet of learning power works.
6. This shades into prompting, which at first might need to involve some rather heavy-handed hints, and gradually fades into the merest nudge or a raised eyebrow.
7. Finally, your work as a coach is done, with respect to that particular aspect of learning power, when the skill or inclination manifests itself automatically when it is needed, without the student having to think consciously about it.

Teaching for transfer

BLP teachers want the learning power that students are developing to be available to them not only in the context of the maths or history lesson in which they learned and practised it; they want it to show up when needed in real life as well. But teaching for this degree of generalisation or transfer is not as easy as you might think. It doesn't just happen. Many programmes aimed at teaching thinking skills or creativity have had disappointing results. They often get an enthusiastic reception, but then they fail to materialise when they are needed, they fail to spread, and they fail to last.

To get learning power to seep into young people's approach to learning across the board, you have to do three things. First, they have to practise the different elements of learning power in different subject areas. If they only ever think about **resilience** in science, or **reflectiveness** in English, then the ability, however well it has developed, is likely to stay stuck to that domain, and will only be triggered by it. Second, you have to extend the range of examples beyond the context of school—if only through discussion and imagination. You have to ask students regularly 'When could you use making links in real life?', or 'What do you do in your sports training where managing distractions is relevant?' Beyond that, you have to get them into the habit of looking for these links themselves, and suggesting them spontaneously. Third, you have to keep talking with students about the overall framework of learning power, and about its general relevance to daily life, so that they get used to thinking in the language of learning power as they go about their lives.

Section 4
Beyond the classroom

The BLP approach doesn't just affect what goes on in the classroom. It can permeate the whole life of the school—and becomes much more effective when it does so. In this section, we offer some ideas about how BLP can infuse the rest of students' school life, the behind-the-scenes world of teachers, and the school's relationships with the wider community.

Quality Circle Time

One approach that pays particular attention to students' experiences during breaks and lunchtimes is the Whole School Quality Circle Time approach pioneered by Jenny Mosley in Wiltshire primary schools, and now widely used throughout the UK. At the core of the approach is a concern with students' social and emotional well-being, and the regular practice of 'circle time' during which students learn how to express their feelings and listen to others more effectively. These meetings are embedded within a whole-school approach that includes an agreed system of behaviour expectations (the 'Golden Rules') and incentives and sanctions to keep them in place. Attention is also paid to teachers' sense of emotional well-being, and to the role that all teaching assistants, lunchtime supervisors, administrative and other support staff can play. Talking especially of the importance of carrying through good intentions into break times, Mosley writes:

'Many children's behavioural problems stem from the fact that they do not know how to play with each other. Break times can be experiences of fear, loneliness and boredom. Feelings of being left out or picked on can be engendered and exacerbated. Those who supervise these breaks can feel beleaguered in the face of noisy, aggressive or frustrated children. Good practice means creating possibilities for all kids to join in a range of different activities. It also means providing quiet places for them to go . . . The model insists that schools teach playground games, and 'zones' the playground into activity areas that can be supervised by older children . . . Lunchtime supervisors are given the same rights as teachers, and are encouraged to use the same incentive and sanction system . . .'

Alice Witherow, Deputy Head at a very difficult school in Essex that has successfully used the Quality Circle Time approach, says that paying attention to what goes on at lunchtimes was an important part of their strategy. 'We have organised areas of the playground for specific activities. Teachers help with playground games, and there is equipment available for children to play with. There is also an opportunity for children to come off the playground and work with an assistant on playing games and making things. An allotment is available where plants can be grown.'

Circle Time is now being used in more and more secondary schools, as well as primaries. Evaluations reveal that the approach does not just develop students' 'emotional literacy': it helps to develop their learning power in a number of ways. Both teachers and students say it has a major impact on reciprocity. Students quickly become much better at speaking, listening and waiting their turn. They work better together. But it also improves resilience, resourcefulness and reflectiveness. Students concentrate better and try harder to learn. They develop a more 'can do' attitude. And they learn to talk and think more fluently about themselves as learners as well. 93% of Wiltshire Headteachers agreed that circle time had a positive influence on learning. 87% thought that it helped students to recognise their own abilities. And 99% believed that circle time (for both students and staff) had had a positive effect on the overall ethos of the school.

Beyond the classroom

In the previous section, we focused on individual teachers in their classrooms. This is, as we said, the engine-room of the approach. But BLP does not stop when the bell goes. It really comes into its own when it begins to infuse the whole life of the school, and percolate out into the wider community. We might divide these areas beyond the classroom into three: students' experience of School Life more generally; the behind-the-scenes World of Teachers as learners, managers and professionals; and relations with the Wider Community of which the school is part. Before we conclude, let's just say a word about each of these.

The same four general processes that were at work in the classroom are influential in these areas as well. Some direct **explaining** to both teaching and support staff is essential. The quality of their informal conversation and **commentary** on students' activities as they go around the school, and on each others' ups and downs, sets the general tone as to whether it is safe, or encouraged, to be a learner in this school. The way activities are **orchestrated** for students (e.g. games and clubs), teachers (meetings and reviews), and members of the outside community (parents' evenings, out-of-hours use of the facilities) all convey powerful messages about learning. And, of course, what teachers **model** to students, visitors and each other also has a major impact.

School Life

The BLP approach can manifest itself in all the other aspects of school life that are experienced by the students. These are important for they can act as bridges between the learning-to-learn that takes place in the context of the formal curriculum and less structured or less content-focused aspects of their lives. These include the way things are talked about in assemblies; what is displayed on the corridor walls and in the foyer; the role of playground and lunchtime supervisors; the way extra-curricular activities are offered; the kinds of interactions between older and younger students that are encouraged. All of these go to make up the overall ethos of the school as experienced by the students, and they either reinforce or undermine the learning power that is being cultivated in the classroom.

Assemblies

Not all students attend an 'assembly' every day, but most have such a get-together at least once a week. How is this time spent, and what are the messages about the school that are celebrated or reinforced? In some schools it is a time for recognising good or bad conduct—'Well done those Year 10 boys for their help in the High Street. Worrying stories about harassment of late-night shoppers in the supermarket car park.' But there are opportunities to celebrate learning, instead of good or bad performance or

Beyond the classroom . . .

achievement. Both staff and students could make brief presentations of a current project (with its failures, false starts, warts and all). The inspiring stories that are told could be stories of resilience, resourcefulness, reflectiveness and reciprocity in learning, as well as of helpfulness or success.

Displays

What would there be on the walls and in the foyer of a BLP school? Would the corridors be lined with examples of the most beautifully produced students' work—implicitly recognising achievement—or would there be displays that reveal the uncertain process of learning? If the latter, we might be more likely to find scribbled-on drafts of poems and essays, a messy lab note-book, or a project abandoned, with a note explaining that the author had had a much better idea. Or there might be a big 'graffiti board' for suggestions about future learning activities, or an 'information exchange', where people offer to trade knowledge and skills: 'Veejay in 8B wants to learn how to juggle, and will offer tuition on his PlayStation 2 in return.' 'Miss Philippousis needs help with level 3 Tetris; offers introductory Greek or CeRoc lessons in exchange.' There are any number of ways in which the physical spaces could be used to promote the message that this is a place passionately interested in development and improvement, and not afraid to display the processes of exploration and inquiry that such growth involves.

Support staff

What are students allowed or encouraged to get up to in their playtime and lunch break? What kinds of values do the playground and lunchtime supervisors display, as they tend to students' physical needs and oversee their safety? What balance between good manners, creative play and personal safety do their words and their body language betoken? Are there opportunities to discuss what the school policy on learning-to-learn in these extra-curricular contexts might be? There are plenty of opportunities to involve support staff in the BLP philosophy. Some schools automatically involve their support staff in their professional development activities, but not all do. Do support staff get a chance to talk to students about their own learning stories? The caretaker and the cleaners probably have fascinating tales to tell about the way that they have met some of the challenges and confusions of their life.

Extra-curricular activities

Students who take part in out-of-school (but organised-by-school) activities subsequently do better in life on a whole raft of measures (see page 112). Because such activities are voluntary, they may recruit a higher level of responsibility and engagement, and so develop concentration and stickability. They may also develop different 'learning muscles' from those habitually exercised in the classroom—learning through direct experience, through imagination and through intuition, for example. These kinds of activities build up especially the fourth R, reciprocity. As the research shows, in extra-curricular activities, young people learn to learn from and with each other to a greater extent than is possible in many lessons, and this stands them in good stead when they go out into a very team-oriented world of work (as well, of course, as the world of relationships itself).

School council

A students' school council typically has some responsibility for discussing issues, making recommendations and even taking decisions that affect the running of the school. It is also a forum in which students' perceptions and concerns can be voiced, and fed through to leaders and managers in the school. But the extent to which such discussions promote the development of the four Rs depends critically on how much responsibility students are given, and how meetings are organised and run. Of course there are limits to what responsibilities it is proper or appropriate to delegate to such a council. There is no point in raising students' expectations and inviting their opinions about matters which it is impossible to respond to. Students, like teachers, are sensitive to tokenism. But such a forum not only encourages ownership of and commitment to the ideals and activities of the school; it can offer valuable practice in the four Rs, encouraging perseverance, questioning, reasoning, planning and listening, amongst others.

Homework

Homework is an outpost of School World that the students take home with them. It is not just an opportunity for teachers to get students to consolidate the specific subject-matter they have been working on in class. It is an opportunity for students to practise their learning strategies and attitudes in a new setting, and to develop the confidence and capacity to know their own learning habits and organise their learning world independently. But if this is to happen it needs scaffolding and reviewing. Students could be asked to experiment with the conditions under which they do their studying—how do different kinds of noise, such as music, TV, or adults' chatter, impact on their concentration or their creativity? They might be invited to write a few notes about what they have found, and/or to contribute to a discussion at the start of the next lesson in school. Over time, the teacher could work through the different aspects of learning power, using homework to focus attention on them individually and in combination.

Vertical grouping

One of the key ideas behind reciprocity is that people learn a lot about learning simply from working alongside each other, modelling and imitating their learning styles and strategies. Just as students can pick up more powerful ways of thinking from their teachers, so they can from each other. One way to maximise this unspoken transfer is for students of different ages to work and play together. So-called vertical grouping is not just a way of getting students to look after each other (by creating a kind of 'family' structure for part of the day); it is a way of helping their learning power develop too. In the Belaya Kalitva Golden Key School, for example, students spend the first and last 45 minutes of each day in stable groups of about a dozen people (including a teacher). The students range in age from three to twelve. At the end of the school day, they are encouraged to make links in their minds between what has happened during the day, and what they will take home to their families. As they do so, the little ones pick up the ways in which the elder students tell their stories, frame questions, and interact with one another.

Regrets about a lack of involvement . . .

Leah Dixon, a 25-year-old graduate living in north London, regrets not having involved herself in more extra-curricular activities both at school and university. 'I've come out of so many years of education without the confidence and skill or knowledge to know what I would like to do or what I'd be good at', she said (in an interview in *The Independent*, 25 September, 2000). 'Being part of clubs or writing for the university paper might have helped me to know what I wanted to do later in life. Joining a debating society or speaking in front of the school at 16 would have made walking into a boardroom less intimidating . . . You find the people who are successful are those people who were motivated in school because they managed to get motivated outside of school as well.'

RESEARCH TELLS US . . .

Extra-curricular activities build learning for life

In 2000, Professor Bonnie Barbie of the University of Arizona published the results of a sixteen year study of the effects on students' later lives of their involvement, while they were at school, in activities like clubs, sports, community work, and musical and dramatic productions. 2,200 young people were tracked through from age 11 to 27. Not only were students who took part in these activities likely to do better academically than their more bookish peers; they also felt better prepared to set their own goals and learn independently later on.

Says Professor Barbie: 'These extra-curricular activities extend a richness of possibilities a teenager wouldn't get just by attending school and doing homework with no outside interests.' She suggests that the most important factor at work is reciprocity: in the context of such activities, young people learn a great deal from each other, and build up the skills and the confidence to work and learn better with other people.

Beyond the classroom . . .

Teachers' World

The BLP approach can influence a great deal of what goes on in the teachers' world of planning, professional development, management, leadership and meetings. There are many aspects of the teachers' world that have a significant impact on whether learning-to-learn is happening throughout the school, or not. They include the extent to which teachers are encouraged to learn from and with each other; the school's informal culture of judgement about experiment and innovation; the nature of more formal staff performance review; policy and practice towards professional development; the conduct and ownership of staff meetings; the process of policy development and monitoring; and the quality of leadership. Let's take a brief look at each of these.

Peer learning

For the BLP approach, it is both highly desirable to have a body of teachers who are not just enthusiastic about students' learning-to-learn, but about their own. Staff who see themselves as willing learners, and interested in becoming better at their own learning (both personal and professional) are going to be better role models for the students, and more willing to try out ways of developing the fours Rs in their classrooms. Peer observation is an effective way of helping teachers develop a collaborative learning culture. Giving strong encouragement for teachers to open their classrooms and their practices to each other can open up a general climate of discussion and debate about the various learning methods in use around the school. Formally arranged systems of mentoring and peer coaching can also speed the dissemination of good practice throughout the school.

Action research

Perhaps the most common kind of teacher learning, much in fashion at present, is to undertake a piece of action research or classroom inquiry on some aspect of their own practice. It is easy to focus these on the quality of learning that is being encouraged in the classroom. For example:

- 'Do I respond differently to boys and girls when they are stuck or give a wrong answer? Does that affect the level of stickability I am getting from them?'
- 'Would it improve the quality of their ideas if I trained them in how to use visualisation techniques?'
- 'Would playing "Spot the deliberate mistake" games help the low-achieving boys check their own maths problems better?'

Planning this kind of self-observation, and collecting the right kind of data, are quite high-level research skills, and can often be supported by a friendly local education lecturer or an adviser from the LEA. Such studies have a cumulative effect not just on the individual teacher but on the culture of the school as a whole (see the quote on page 116).

Beyond the classroom . . .

Informal judgement

Perhaps the strongest inhibitor of learning amongst a school staff is if it is seen as uncool or unsafe. It can be very hard to engage in innovation, or show enthusiasm for new ideas, when the prevailing staffroom culture is jaded or cynical. In the worst cases, any form of enthusiasm or participation can be stigmatised by powerful opinion-leaders as 'immature'. Inexperienced teachers, especially, who may have a good deal of energy and creativity to offer, may not dare to experiment if a temporarily noisy classroom is automatically seen as reflecting a lack of competence. It behoves other powerful figures in the school, particularly the leadership team, to do what they can to make cynicism objectionable, not learning. They should use all four of the learning channels—explaining, commentating, orchestrating and modelling—to try to shift the culture, where it is needed.

Performance management

Although the climate of informal judgement is most important, there may be a place for a small amount of 'stick and carrot' to encourage teachers to be learners. For example, their own learning could constitute one element of performance management, in which teachers take stock not just of what they have learnt, and where they might go next, but of how their learning is going, and what BLP target they might like to set for themselves. (Several companies, British Aerospace for one, take a regular self, peer and manager-based inventory of their middle managers' development of key areas of capability and attitude, of which three are resilience, innovative thinking and team membership.) Eligibility for further support (or even for the contentious upper pay-spine awards) could be assessed in part on teachers' commitment to their own learning.

Professional development

But if staff are to become more involved in their own learning-to-learn, they need the support and resources to do so. This could be through a formal programme of professional development, or otherwise. Encouragement to engage in higher degree work—and to make it known to the students that teachers are expected to be learners too—can have a major impact on school ethos. There are several forms that this learning can take. It might be to sign up for a masters' course in education. It might be to undertake some further study of their own curriculum subject. An adventurous head—as some commercial companies do—might even support a proposal to undertake some learning project that is of personal interest but which has no direct (but hopefully plenty of indirect) benefit to the work of the school.

Staff meetings

The way meetings are arranged and run has a big impact on how willing their members are to talk about their own learning. I have heard of a head who insisted that he genuinely wanted to hear people's suggestions, and when one junior member of staff was foolish enough to venture one, paused for an icy moment and said: 'Now, has anyone got any sensible suggestions?' Such responses do not make for a vibrant learning community. Nor do meetings where it rapidly becomes clear that discussions are a waste of time because decisions have already been made. On the positive side, some BLP schools make a point of protecting 'brainstorming' time in their meetings, and of routinely showcasing one department's innovations in their teaching to the rest of the staff. However the meeting is structured, recruiting people's active engagement is just as much a prerequisite for teachers' learning as it is for students'.

Policy development

A major role of the school's leadership is to propose changes to the structures and procedures—the policy—of the school. The nature of the timetable, of year groupings, of communication and committee structures, and a dozen other aspects of school life are not cast in stone. Some of the ideas we have suggested earlier might lead the leadership team towards considering a vertical structure of mixed-age 'home groups', for example. Time might be found in Years 7 and 8 for a much more intensive focus on learning-to-learn, at the expense of some traditional curriculum time. (One leadership team of a large comprehensive school, for example, decided they would require department heads to come up with plans for saving 10% of their curriculum teaching time in Year 7, so that a real foundation of learning skills and attitudes could be laid.) Along similar lines, several schools have managed to free up a day a fortnight, say—some call it Day 10—for the whole school, staff and students, to engage in day-long learning projects of any kind. Anyone can offer a 'class' in whatever they like, and anyone can sign up for it.

Policy decisions are needed to make sure that the BLP approach carries through from year to year. A few isolated BLP teachers can have a positive effect on their students' learning power, but the effect is amplified enormously if each teacher can build upon what their colleagues are doing. A Year 10 class is ready to tackle much more ambitious learning targets if they have been used to the language and the approach since their primary school days.

Monitoring

One of the responsibilities of any effective management team is to collect regular information that enables them to see the extent to which (a) what has been agreed is actually being done, and (b) it is having the desired (positive) effect on learning and teaching. How this information is collected, and what information is required, depends on—amongst other things—the policy commitment to BLP. A useful exercise, especially at the point where the BLP approach is being considered and debated, is to devise a way of checking the 'vital signs' of the school as a BLP community already—what we call the Learning Amble. Trying to devise such a set of indicators is a very useful exercise, for it forces staff to think concretely about what their version of BLP is trying to achieve, and how they would recognise it if it happened.

Leadership

We see BLP leadership as concerning the way in which respected figures in the school demonstrate and embody their commitment to learning-to-learn, and their willingness and ability to reveal

Learner-teachers

When Tamsyn Imison took over as head of Hampstead School in North London, she found herself in a situation very different from the leafy middle-class image that the name of the school might suggest. Fewer than half of the school's 1300 intake spoke English as their first language. Five years later, the school had been transformed, with more than 50% of GCSE candidates getting five or more good grades. One of Tamsyn's main strategies was to get as many teachers as possible involved in their own learning, with, for example, a local university delivering an MA programme to 14 teachers on-site. And she made sure that the students knew that their teachers were being learners. 'If you want continuing improvement in a school, you have to have a learning culture,' she says, 'It sends a message to the children that we really care about learning, too. We want them to do as we do, not just as we say.'

> One of the most interesting activities we observed in [our] school improvement program was the change in staff attitudes and actions relating to what we call inquiry-mindedness. Over the years, many of them have become quite adept not only at collecting data but, much more importantly, at thinking about it, interpreting it in context and using it wisely . . . They were no longer in awe of data, neither were they looking for data to confirm their prejudices nor endorse their practices. Instead they were actively searching for understanding, struggling to describe the complexity of their work, and using systematic inquiry procedures to stand back and think about their school.
>
> Lorna Earl and Linda Lee, 'The Manitoba School Improvement Program'

Beyond the classroom . . .

themselves as learners. Where management is about enabling, encouraging and evaluating other people, leadership is more about how people 'walk the talk' themselves. However, to shift from seeing yourself as headteacher or chief executive to head learner is not easy, and not without its pitfalls. Parents, governors and staff may have well-established expectations that it is your competence and firm grasp that earns you your position and your salary, not your willingness to admit your uncertainty. In the face of such judgements, leaders may need to prepare the ground more thoroughly for their shift in priorities.

But above that, BLP leaders, whether in private or in public, need to be open to their own learning. They need to be reflective: interested in mulling over their experiences and learning from them, in talking to peers openly, in reading around the job, and perhaps in keeping a reflective journal. And, of course, leadership is not just an issue for heads and deputies. Everyone in the school is capable of being a lead learner. Five-year-olds are perfectly capable of being role models of 'confident uncertainty', just as much as the headteacher. Teaching assistants can model resilience and resourcefulness as well as a head of year. The idea that everyone in the school is capable of sharing the responsibility for showing what it means to 'walk the talk' of BLP may start with the headteacher, but it can quickly work its way throughout every cell of the body.

The Wider Community

The final set of ways in which the school can support the BLP approach is through its dealings with the wider community of which it is part, and with the outside world in general. It is a core aim of BLP that young people develop learning power not just so that they can do school learning more easily and effectively, but so that they will leave school with a general-purpose set of habits and attitudes which will serve them well in all areas of life. In order to achieve this second aim, it is important that as many bridges as possible are built between the school and the outside world. The more permeable the boundaries, the more likely the sought-after transfer is to occur. Some of the relevant areas are: how the school communicates about BLP with parents, and recruits their support; the relationship with the governors; involvement of members of the local community; and networking with other schools and agencies, both in person and via the internet.

Parents

Schools sometimes have an ambivalent relationship with parents, but they can be both a tremendous support for the school's BLP policies, and a great source of learning power coaching in their own right. First, they need to have the ideas explained to them, and to have the opportunity to ask questions and express concerns. Once they understand what is involved, and what is at stake, my experience is that the overwhelming response is: How can we help? Here are some suggestions.

Beyond the classroom . . .

- Obviously welcome and foster your child's questioning spirit, as much as you can.
- Give young children interesting things to figure out, or, preferably encourage them to learn about what spontaneously interests *them*. Don't rush to protect them too soon from difficulty. (Do just enough to get them going again when they are stuck; don't take it as an opportunity to finish the jigsaw puzzle yourself, or to explain at great length your pet theory about why the sky is blue.)
- Notice, and help them to notice, when they are operating (even if only for a moment) at the leading edge of their resilience, resourcefulness and so on. (But don't fall into the trap of praising them too lavishly, or they may become hooked on the praise rather than the joy of learning for its own sake.)
- Start a scrapbook of your child's learning moments, and look over it occasionally with them to remind them how much they have progressed.
- Involve them in your own learning activities, even if only as interested observers, and try to 'think aloud' as you try out a new recipe or struggle with a bit of DIY.

Children, especially young children, learn a great deal from eavesdropping on adults and observing them as they go about their learning and problem-solving. Children are designed to be little apprentices, and they will happily apprentice themselves to anyone they like who is doing something interesting—whether that be arguing, looking for something they have lost, reacting to bad news, or making a curry. Even watching you struggle a bit is good learning. Parents are not omniscient or omnipotent, and it helps children grow if they can be privy to some of their elders' uncertainties: not when they are falling apart, but when they are floundering just a little.

Governors

The 'head learner' of a school obviously needs to get the governors, and other influential local figures, on their side. They too need time to assimilate what the BLP approach is, and why it is necessary for the next generation to grow up as good learners. They may need to be reassured by being shown the research which demonstrates that the conventional indicators of school success are also much more likely to go up than down. Once recruited, governors are often enthusiastic about the opportunity to be learning role models themselves, talking to the students about their own learning world, as well as using their contacts to create useful links into the local community.

Local business and community

Local employers and business people can be invited into learning partnerships with the school. There is a vast pool of interesting real-life learners in the community who could come more regularly into school to tell of their experiences, and to demonstrate what the behind-the-scenes learning processes and tribulations are of a midwife, a sculptor, a rock musician or a shopkeeper. It may also be possible to increase the traffic in the other direction. There are examples already where school students offer genuine research consultancy to local enterprises. Once students have mastered a range of research skills—library and internet searches, basic statistical analyses, collating and reporting information and so on—they can be of real use to businesses in helping them to research some of their problems. In this kind of win-win relationship, businesses might even be willing to make contributions to the school (financial or otherwise), and students are able to practise and hone their skills. Engagement always tends to be greater when students feel they are doing something real. And of course many schools are already exploring ways in which they can develop their role as community learning centres. Adults are welcome in lessons to learn alongside the younger students, and the facilities are made available to community groups outside the normal school day.

Networking

There are many useful ways in which schools can network with other schools, either in the local area or further afield, through the wonders of e-mail and the internet. There are many schemes already in existence where students work on joint research projects with networks of other schools, comparing environmental or meteorological conditions around the world, or sharing folk tales from different countries. Learning to use electronic media for these discussions—not only e-mail but video-conferencing, for example—is as useful a preparation for the world of work as they are likely to find it. Teachers too can learn a lot from networking with other schools. After they have been in a school for a while, they may become so enculturated that they forget how differently things are done elsewhere. Visits to and from other schools may open up opportunities for development which might otherwise never have been considered. There are also advantages of peer relationships between teachers who are not part of the same school team. Headteachers often derive great benefit from sharing experiences and dilemmas with other heads in the region.

E-mail opens up possibilities for conversations between the members of a school, both staff and students, and other institutions of education such as colleges and universities. There are many schemes in the UK, the USA and elsewhere, where undergraduates gain credits for working with schools (either on line or face-to-face), or where graduate students or lecturers are willing to offer opinions and information in response to e-mail queries from school students. Again, such e-conversations strengthen both students' confidence and their communication skills.

It will be obvious by now that the BLP approach can shape every aspect of a school's aims and activities. From an informal word to a struggling student, to the display in the foyer, from playground supervision to the use of the internet: in a hundred different ways, a school is either creating opportunities to build learning power or neglecting to do so. We hope that you will want to find out more about how BLP could work in your school or college.

SELF-ESTEEM

Further reading

Carole Aimes. 'Classrooms: Goals, Structures and Student Motivation.' *Journal of Educational Psychology* 84 (1992): 261–71.

John Baird and Jeff Northfield. *Learning from the PEEL Experience.* Melbourne, Australia: Monash University Press, 1992.

Tom Bentley. *Learning Beyond the Classroom: Education for a Changing World.* London: RoutledgeFalmer, 1998.

John Bransford, Ann Brown and Rodney Cocking. *How People Learn: Brain, Mind, Experience and School.* Washington DC: National Academy Press, 1999.

Ann Brown. 'Transforming Schools into Communities of Thinking and Learning about Serious Matters.' *American Psychologist* 52 (1997): 399–413.

Cardiff Schools Service. *Learning to Learn: Enquiries into Building Resourceful, Resilient and Reflective Learners.* Cardiff: Cardiff County Council, 2002.

Guy Claxton. *Wise Up: The Challenge of Lifelong Learning.* London and New York: Bloomsbury, 1999. Stafford: Network Educational Press, 2001.

Mihaly Csikszentmihalyi. *Flow: The Psychology of Optimal Experience.* San Francisco: HarperPerennial, 1990.

Laura Earl & Linda Lee. 'Learning for a Change: School Improvement as Capacity Building.' *Improving Schools* 3 (2000): 30–38.

Howard Gardner. *The Unschooled Mind: How Children Think and How Schools Should Teach.* New York: Basic Books, 1991.

Daniel Goleman. *Emotional Intelligence: Why It Can Matter More than IQ.* London: Bloomsbury, 1996.

Rachel Jupp. *What Learning Needs: The Challenge for a Creative Nation.* London: Demos, 2001.

Ellen Langer. *The Power of Mindful Learning.* New York: Addison-Wesley, 1997.

Bill Lucas and Toby Greany. *Schools in the Learning Age.* London: Campaign for Learning, 2000.

Bill Lucas, Toby Greany, Jill Rodd and Ray Wicks. *Teaching Pupils how to Learn.* Stafford: Network Educational Press, 2002.

Barbara McCombs and Jo Sue Whisler. *The Learner-Centered Classroom and School.* San Francisco: Jossey-Bass, 1997.

Jenny Mosley. *Quality Circle Time: The Heart of the Curriculum.* Trowbridge, Wilts: Positive Press, 2000.

David Perkins. *Smart Schools: Better Thinking and Learning for Every Child.* New York: The Free Press, 1992.

Ken Richardson. *The Making of Intelligence.* London: Phoenix, 2000.

Peter Senge and others. *Schools that Learn: A Fifth Discipline Fieldbook.* London: Nicholas Brealey, 2000.

Alistair Smith & Nicola Call. *The ALPS Approach: Accelerated Learning in Primary Schools.* Stafford: Network Educational Press, 1999.

Geoff Southworth. 'How Primary Schools Learn.' *Research Papers in Education* 15 (2000), 275–91.

Louise Stoll, Dean Fink & Laura Earl. *It's About Learning (And It's About Time).* London: RoutledgeFalmer, 2002.

Jeannette Vos and Gordon Dryden. *The Learning Revolution.* Stafford: Network Educational Press, 2001.

Chris Watkins. *Learning about Learning Enhances Performance.* Research Matters, no. 13. London: Institute of Education, 2001.

Chris Watkins and others. *Effective Learning.* Research Matters, no. 17. London: Institute of Education, 2002.